Heinemann ECONOMICS AS *for Edexcel*

Heinemann

ECONOMICS AS

for Edexcel

BY

Sue Grant *and* Chris Vidler

with Andrew Ellams

heinemann.co.uk
✓ Free online support
✓ Useful weblinks
✓ 24 hour online ordering

01865 888058

Inspiring generations

Heinemann Educational Publishers
Halley Court, Jordan Hill, Oxford OX2 8EJ
Part of Harcourt Education

Heinemann is the registered trademark of
Harcourt Education Limited

First published 2003

07 06 05 04 03
10 9 8 7 6 5 4 3 2 1

British Library Cataloguing in Publication Data is available
from the British Library on request.

ISBN 0 435 33082 9

Designed by Artistix

Typeset by Hardlines Ltd, Charlbury, Oxford

Original illustrations © Harcourt Education Limited 2003
Illustrated by Hardlines Ltd, Charlbury, Oxford

Cover design by Matt Buckley

Printed and bound in the UK, by The Bath Press

Picture research by Sally Cole

Acknowledgements

The publishers would like to thank the following for
permission to use photographs: Sean Aidan/Eye
Ubiquitous, p. 47; Bennet/Dean/Eye Ubiquitous, p 34;
Bettman/Corbis, p102; Robert Brook/Photofusion, p. 85;
John Cole, p. 136; EPA Press/Press Association, pp. 34,
72; Mary Evans, p. 43; Jim Hodson/Photofusion, p. 78;
Charles O'Rear/Corbis, p. 119; Lee S. Pascal/Corbis, p. 91;
Press Association, p. 86 J. Stilwell/Press association,
p. 143.

Every effort has been made to contact copyright holders
of material reproduced in this book. Any omissions will
be rectified in subsequent printings if notice is given to
the publishers.

Websites

Links to appropriate websites are given throughout the
pack. Although these were up-to-date at the time of
writing, it is essential for teachers to preview these sites
before using them with pupils. These will ensure that the
web address (URL) is still accurate and the content is
suitable for your needs.

We suggest that you bookmark useful sites and consider
enabling pupils to access them through the school
intranet. We are bringing this to your attention as we are
aware of legitimate sites being appropriated illegally by
people wanting to distribute unsuitable and offensive
material. We strongly advise you to purchase suitable
screening software so that pupils are protected from
unsuitable sites and their material.

If you do find that the links given no longer work, or the
content is unsuitable, please let us know. Details of
changes will be posted on our website.

The express code for this book is 0829P.

Tel: 01865 888058 www.heinemann.co.uk

Contents

Introduction

Welcome to AS economics. This book as been specially written for students taking the Edexcel course. This means that it:

- follows the Edexcel specification very closely
- has been written to ensure that all concepts are clearly explained in terms understandable by students taking this subject for the first time
- includes lots of advice written by examiners to help you get the best possible grade.

You might already be an expert

For many of you, this will be the first time you have studied economics for a formal qualification. This does not mean to say that you know nothing about the subject. All of us have a basic understanding of many of the concepts that, when put together, make up economics. Thus, you will know that prices go up if there is a shortage of something that people wish to buy. You will also know that if the reverse were to happen, prices are likely to fall. Similarly if there is only one supplier of a particular good, customers may be forced to pay more than if lots of different companies are competing for our custom. You did know that, didn't you?

You probably also realise that governments play a big part in influencing the provision of many services like health, education and housing, and that these are financed by the taxes we pay. It follows that if the government has to spend more in order to build more hospitals or increase the number of nurses and doctors, this could mean cutting spending elsewhere (on defence, for example), raising more in taxation, or, perhaps less obviously, borrowing more money. The point here is that someone somewhere will have to pay for such improvements.

Getting to grips with economics

Learning economics will change your life. It will alter the way you see and understand the world. Watching TV, reading newspapers, listening and taking part in conversations will be not be the same again. So what is this 'new' subject all about?

We all learn things in different ways, so it is hard to be too prescriptive about the best ways of getting to grips with economics. Its special technical vocabulary can be a big barrier, especially when different meanings are given to words that we commonly use. But, once learnt, the vocabulary is a real shortcut to understanding. Also, there are some diagrams and simple maths involved in understanding economics concepts.

However, on the plus side, nothing in economics is cut and dried. Economics is about the stuff all around us – about life, in fact. It will help you understand the world as we know it, and studying economics can involve lots of argument and debate.

Web links

Advice on using the Internet can be found by going to the following website and entering express code 0829P: www.heinemann.co.uk/hotlinks.

All that can be said is that *beginning* your study of economics is usually the hardest stage. Once you get over the initial differentness of the subject, it can be fun and really useful. Economics should help you to think and argue more logically, and these skills are really valued in the marketplace for jobs. Thus, qualifications in economics usually carry more status and value than qualifications in many other subjects. So hang in there, even when it seems tough. It will be worth it in the end. Incidentally, AS economics has one of the highest progression rates from AS to A2. In other words, a large majority of students who take AS go on to take the full A' level. Now, that must say something for the subject!

An economic perspective

So what is special about economics? Economics exists because we live in a world in which resources are finite. There are not endless supplies of energy, minerals, foodstuffs and so on.

On the other hand, we live in a world in which the vast majority of people are materialistic in the sense of always wanting more. Two-thirds of the world's population don't have enough to eat. Most of us aspire to improving our lifestyles by having more and better and newer and nicer things. In short, people have unlimited wants. Their needs outstrip the means of satisfying them. Put simply, threes into two won't go. There is not enough to go round. Some people starve, while others enjoy fantastic standards of luxury.

This is not a morality tale. Rather, it is a description of the world in which we live. Economists use this image to demonstrate the fundamentals of their subject. Economics is about making choices. People have virtually unlimited wants. Resources are finite. Economics is about making more informed choices. It is about understanding that if one choice is made, others have to be forgone. For example, it can be argued that if we want cleaner air, then we need to use cars less. This sacrifice is called an opportunity cost – that is, what has to be given up as the result of a particular choice.

We can't always get what we want. Therefore, all societies need some kind of economic system in order to decide what gets produced, how it is produced and, crucially, who gets what. Unravelling and understanding these sort of issues is what economics is all about, and learning about the subject gives a better understanding of the forces that have and will shape all our lives.

Starting to think like an economist: positive versus normative

We all know about economics. We are all consumers and producers. All of us argue, knowingly and unknowingly, about economic issues. People have views about immigration, the destruction of rain forests or restrictions on tobacco advertising. Different values lead to different views of what is right and wrong, and what governments and others ought to do. This kind of thinking

Economics exists because in the world we live in we have to make choices. Wants are said to be infinite, whereas resources are finite.

Positive economics involves the collection of evidence that can be used to support or challenge theories and statements. Normative economics is more to do with people's values and beliefs.

is often referred to as normative economics. However, economics is about more than having views on a range of controversial issues. It is a social science, and the term 'positive economics' is used to describe an approach to economics that is more objective and emphasises the use and value of:

- key economic theories
- evidence
- a specialist technical vocabulary.

Theories and concepts

Economics as we know it today has developed over the last 400 years. Some would argue that its origins are much older, but recent developments are linked with industrialisation and the development of capitalism. Adam Smith, who wrote *Wealth of Nations* in 1776, is seen as one of the first economists. He wrote about how specialisation in particular tasks could lead to greater production. As with other disciplines, the subject has constantly evolved and successive generations of economists have argued and debated each other's work. In this way, a body of knowledge and understanding associated with economics has developed. There is broad agreement about parts of this and dispute about others.

Evidence

Evidence is used to support or refute economic theories. Economists are, therefore, often concerned with the collection of numerical and other data, but in relation to human behaviour. You can't subject people to strict laboratory conditions, but at the same time theories and concepts should be based on the careful collection of evidence. This means that numerical data is very important, as is the development of logical and ordered argument.

Technical vocabulary

As with all disciplines, economics has a technical vocabulary all of its own. Economists are also very precise in their use of particular terms. This precise use of particular terms takes some getting used to but it is important, especially in terms of clearly communicating your understanding of the subject and developing economic analysis and argument.

Note: The *Definitions* in the page margins throughout this book for help and support in learning this vocabulary (see also the Glossary, pages 163–70).

Positive economics

Objectivity, the application of theory supported by evidence and precise use of a technical vocabulary are all characteristics of what we call positive economics. Economic arguments by politicians, in the newspapers, in the home are often really about people's values – what they believe in and how they think things ought to be. Both approaches are justifiable, but part of the job of the economist is to sort out what is normative and what might be resolved by reference to appropriate evidence.

Quickies

Which of the following could be a normative statement and which a positive?

- The UK ought to join the single currency.
- More trade will take place if the UK joined the single currency.

Course structure

To qualify in AS economics you have to take three examinations. Although these can be taught in different ways, most students will start with the first unit, *Markets – how they work*. This will require you to develop an understanding of how markets work to allocate resources – in other words, why a particular set of goods and services is produced and consumed. Central to understanding *Markets – how they work* is learning about *demand* and *supply*.

The second unit is called the *Markets – why they fail*. As the title implies, economists believe that markets do not always work efficiently or effectively. Thus, if production is in the hands of one supplier, customers may be forced to pay more for the product or service in question. Similarly, markets are linked and what might happen in one market might have an adverse affect on 'innocent' third parties. It is possible for markets to produce too much of something not valued by society or to produce too little of something that is valued.

Finally, *Managing the economy* looks at the whole national economy (rather than individual markets), and involves learning more about inflation, the standard of living and the causes of unemployment. Again, diagrams are used to help you analyse the possible economic effects of changes in things, for instance the impact of 9/11 (the events in the USA that took place on 11 September 2001) or changes in taxation. The 'managing' part of the title refers to the crucial role that governments play when it comes to the working of the whole economy. There should be lots of chances for debate and discussion and you should end up with a much better understanding of things in the news. Although there are clear links between this unit and the other two, you may start it from the beginning of your course.

Finding your way

This book is divided into three parts to reflect the structure of the syllabus outlined above. Part 1 is devoted to markets, Part 2 is about market failure and Part 3 is devoted to managing national economy.

How markets work – an overview

This unit is devoted to microeconomics. In order to do well, you need to understand how individual markets work, the strengths and weaknesses of freely operating markets and how these differ from command, or centrally planned, economies. This involves looking at the changes that have happened in Eastern Europe and provides the basis for tackling the second unit on market failure.

Although there are different ways of organising this module of work, it might be helpful to see it as consisting of three inter-related parts:

- useful concepts
- demand, supply, markets and the price mechanism
- transition in Eastern Europe.

Useful concepts

The course kicks off with what are loosely called 'useful concepts'. These are a mixture of concepts, such opportunity cost, which you will use again and again and that are necessary for you to understand what microeconomics is all about. Guidance is given to help you distinguish between objective statements about economic matters and value judgements, which are more a matter of opinion.

You also need to know about and use production possibility frontiers, which are a very useful tool in helping to judge whether or not economies are working efficiently or not. Other useful concepts include the principle of comparative advantage (which underpins why trade is so important) and consumer and producer surplus (which is a way of analysing the extent to which purchasers and producers gain or lose when market conditions change).

Demand, supply, markets and the price mechanism

You will soon get into the nitty-gritty of what economics is about – in other words, demand and supply. These relate directly to the behaviour of consumers (that's us when we buy goods or services) and producers (which can also be us when we make something or provide a service). However, it is necessary to make a rigid distinction between these two sets of actions. Although there are books and books to underpin the theories of demand and supply, at the end of the day you need to know that it is possible to model the behaviour of consumers and producers using demand and supply curves. Once you have understood this, it will be possible to put these two concepts together to show how markets work to set the price of particular goods or services and also to determine how much is actually sold. This may sound very abstract, but you have only to think of what happens to the prices and sales of lots of goods in the run-up to Christmas and in the January sales.

Individual markets link to each other and chain reactions are set in motion that theoretically allocate resources to those whose demand is strongest. This is known as the price mechanism. Theoretically it should ensure allocative and productive efficiency – in other words, consumers determine what is produced and this is produced at the lowest possible cost. The links between these sections are Illustrated in Figure 1.

Transition economies

One of the special features of the Edexcel course is that you are expected to be able to apply the economics you learn to help understand what is happening in Eastern Europe. In the late 1980s and early 1990s, communist-run governments in countries like Poland, East Germany and Hungary collapsed, as was vividly illustrated by the breaking down of the Berlin Wall. Since then, these governments have been trying to establish what we call mixed economies – that is, ones in which both government and private firms operate to produce the goods and services that are wanted. The final part of this unit encourages you to study these economies in closer detail. The best way of finding out is going there, so lobby your teachers to organise a visit to Prague or Budapest – you won't regret it.

The examination

You will be tested more than once on your understanding of this unit. First, the Unit 1 examination will require you to answer eight 'unit-supported choice questions'. For these you have to choose the most appropriate multiple-choice answer and explain why you have made this choice. Then you have to tackle one of a choice of two data-response questions. For these you are given a short written extract and/or some numerical data, and you are expected to answer four questions, each worth a certain number of marks. The whole exam paper lasts for one hour and, as you have relatively little choice, you have to make sure you have all your knowledge and understanding at your fingertips and use the short time to best advantage.

Don't make the terrible mistake of thinking once this unit is over, you can forget all about demand and supply. Don't throw away your notes. Don't empty your mind of what you have learned. Your understanding of demand and supply will also be tested when you tackle the examination for the second unit, and to varying degrees in all three of your A2 examinations.

Exam tactics

Remember the first unit contributes 30 per cent to your final AS mark, and if you carry on for a second year, 15 per cent of your total A level grade A2. Most importantly, understanding the microeconomics in this unit is the basis for all future study of this subject.

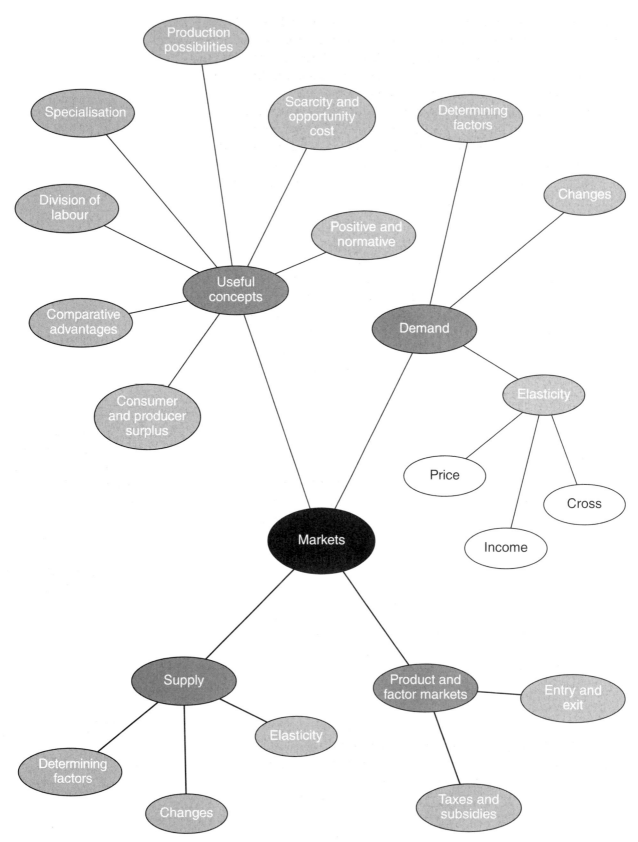

Figure 1

Studying for this unit alone, a typical student will take around 12 weeks to reach the required standard. It will take that long to really get used to demand and supply analysis and its application to different markets. Although you should practise developing your examination techniques from the start, you need a solid grounding in the underpinning theory and concepts before you are fully ready to prepare for the unit tests. Multiple-choice questions will be drawn from the whole of the unit specification, and the data-response questions will assume that you understand the whole of the unit. So don't rush into exam preparation. Work through the activities on pages 52–53 only after you have been through the all sections making up Unit 1, *Markets – how they work.*

Exam timing

Most schools and colleges start their teaching programmes with Unit 1 and it is possible for most students to be ready to take their first AS unit in the January of the first year of their course. But beware; some schools and colleges don't give that option to their students. They argue that too many examinations disrupt too much normal teaching. However, if you have the opportunity, take it. It will get you used to the new demands of AS rather than GCSEs. If you get a good grade, you will become more confident. And even if you don't, you can try again in June.

Tackling this unit

You should try to learn as you go along. Don't be tempted to leave everything to the end. Read each section at least three times – once straight through, a second time to make sure that all the arguments and concepts are really understood, and a final time for reinforcement. Don't do all this at once.

Top tip

Build up a file of contemporary economic events. Get used to reading the business sections of newspapers. Look out for articles about controversial topics, especially if they include up-to-date data. Attach a brief commentary to each – always written with a critical eye.

Revision

Irrespective of how good you are at economics, you can boost your multiple-choice scores by lots of practice. Get hold of all the questions you can and keep going over them. Keep a record of your scores (as percentages). Over time you will get better and better (that's a promise).

Web link

In a very short time you will find that news items in the papers and on TV will make more sense to you. Try to get into the habit of reading the financial sections of newspapers and take advantage of other magazines and periodicals. Go to the website following and type in express code 0829P to find excellent information to support your learning www.heinemann.co.uk/hotlinks.

Hot potato

Brainstorm and agree the ten biggest problems facing the world today. How many are economic?

Factors of production

conomists use the same or similar concepts again and again. Most are easy to understand, but practice needs to be gained in applying them to a range of different contexts. Factors of production are a good example of a simple but powerful concept.

Economics is concerned with a study of how wealth is created. The creation of wealth involves taking resources and transforming them into a product or service that can then be consumed or used in some other way. This process can be illustrated diagrammatically, as shown with a simple input-output model in Figure 1.

This process covers a wide range of issues and concepts important to economists. The input encompasses environmental economics as it deals with the relationship between economic activity and the world's resources, both renewable and finite. The middle part of the model, production, is concerned with how resources are transformed. Business studies students call this process 'adding value', and it can include complex processes involving the use of highly sophisticated technology or the more straightforward harvesting and packaging of an agricultural crop. Finally, the output is the bit concerned with 'shopping' and enjoying or using outputs to improve our lives.

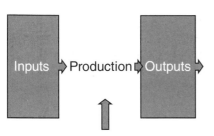

Process of transforming inputs into outputs

Figure 1 Simple input-output model

Definition

The four **factors of production** are: land, labour, capital and enterprise. All outputs consist of varying combinations of each of these inputs.

Types of resources

The simple input-output model shown in Figure 1 can be expanded to identify and classify different types of resources. Economists call these **factors of production** and these are illustrated in Figure 2.

Factors of production

Land

Land includes all that which is locked up in the earth's surface. It includes not just land in the sense of farmland, building and factory sites, but also what are often called 'natural resources', like minerals, fossil fuels and timber, and what can be grown and harvested. Land includes the products of the seas, the content of our atmosphere and, by implication, what has yet to be discovered in space.

Labour

This is a similar 'catch all' concept, which includes what we as people bring to the production process. This includes personal attributes such as strength, individual aptitudes and those skills and capabilities that we can learn.

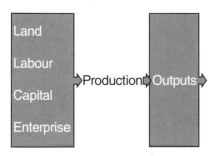

Figure 2 Factors of production

Capital

Economists refer to capital as all those assets that are used to produce goods or services. This category, therefore, includes machinery, factories and equipment that are used to transform 'land' into some particular form of output. The term 'capital' is often used in everyday conversation to describe the money that is used to set up and keep a business going. It is also used to describe savings in shares or such like. All these uses are linked directly or indirectly to the actual production process, but economists use the term 'capital' in a more restricted sense. It could be said that they are not interested in money but the uses to which it can be put, and especially uses that result in economic activity.

Enterprise

This is often described as the fourth factor of production. Economic activity involves the combination of particular quantities of land, labour and capital to produce something. Enterprise is the process of managing and deciding how factors should be confined and to what end. Being enterprising may also involve taking risks and guessing what goods or services are likely to be in demand. Economists consider enterprise as a separate factor of production as it emphasises the importance of decision making within the economy.

Production

So who decides what is actually produced? There is no simple answer to this. All societies are, to varying degrees, mixed economies. They consist of privately owned organisations known as the private sector, national and local governments (confusingly called the public sector) and a range of not-for-profit organisations, which are often charities. These not-for-profit organisations make up the voluntary sector. Put very simply, private sector organisations are considered to be primarily concerned with profit making, the public sector provides services and in the voluntary sector economic activity is not undertaken for financial gain. These are simplifications, as your further study of economics will show, but they provide a starting point for your study.

Making connections

What happens if there is a sudden shortage of capital?

Hot potato

Should entrepreneurs earn more than workers?

Web link

For more information about factors go to: www.heinemann.co.uk/hotlinks and type in express code 0829P.

Quickie ✓

Use the input-output model (Figure 1) to show what happens when beer and crisps are produced.

Production possibility frontiers

Another key economic concept useful in helping you to develop an understanding of economics is that of the production possibility frontier, or curve. (Both terms are used by economists, but Edexcel examiners favour 'frontier' and this is the term used in this book.) This is a graphical technique used to analyse the efficiency of economies.

Understanding production possibility frontiers

In Figure 1 it is assumed that an economy is capable of producing just two goods: corn and beer. If it were to use all its available factors of production to produce corn, it would produce C. Alternatively, if all resources were devoted to making beer, B would be made. The line between C and B is called a production possibility frontier (PPF), because it shows all the different combinations of beer and corn that could be produced. It also illustrates **opportunity cost**, i.e. what has to be given up as the result of a particular decision. For example, the movement from *a* to *b* on the production possibility frontier would indicate an increase in the production of corn. If all resources are being used, this could only be achieved by cutting the production of beer from B1 to B2. This is the opportunity cost of increasing the output of corn.

This form of diagram can be used to represent a variety of changes as illustrated in Figure 2. Thus if a new technique were discovered that meant more beer could be produced using the same amount of resources there would be a movement in the frontier from CB1 to CB2.

This new production possibility frontier indicates a higher possible standard of living, or, as economists would say, a possible increase in wealth which, can be measured as the total value of all that is produced. This society could now produce both more beer and more corn using the same amount of resources.

Point *x* on Figure 2 illustrates an economy that is not making full use of all its resources. Both more beer and more corn could be produced. This illustrates the unemployment of resources and shows how more can be produced with no opportunity cost.

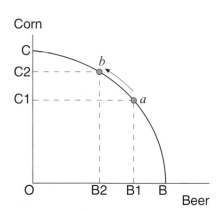

Figure 1 Production possibility frontier

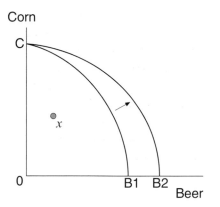

Figure 2 Increasing wealth

Capital and consumer goods

Another useful application of PPFs is in helping to understand the significance of the distinction between capital and consumption goods.

- **Capital goods** are those that are used to produce other goods. Machine tools in a factory are an obvious example.

- **Consumption goods,** on the other hand, are all those things that we consume and use up. You consume drinks, crisps and, maybe, benefit from your teacher's efforts.

The effects of changing the mix in an economy between the production of these two categories of goods can be illustrated using PPFs. In Figure 3, if a country used all of its factors of production to produce capital goods, **P** would be produced. The output of consumption goods would be zero. Alternatively, if all resources were switched, **F** consumption goods could be produced but at a cost of zero production of capital goods. The PPF shows the different combinations of capital and consumption goods that could be produced.

This application is a bit more sophisticated because there is a relationship between the output of capital goods and the output of consumption goods. Greater investment in capital production will mean greater future production of consumption goods. Conversely (the other way round), if the production of capital goods falls below a critical level, the future production of consumption goods will fall. Therefore, it is likely that if a country split production 50/50 between consumption and capital goods (Figure 3, point *a*), in the future its PPF would move outwards from **PF** to **PF1** showing increased economic growth. Alternatively, if only a very small proportion of resources were devoted to the production of capital goods, a future PPF will move inwards indicating a fall in economic growth. This is because all the productive capacity – e.g. machine tools and factories – would eventually wear out and therefore produce fewer consumption goods.

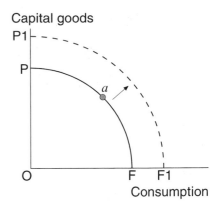

Figure 3 Capital and production good production possibility frontier

Key concept

Any point within a production possibility frontier indicates that some factors of production are not being fully used – i.e. productive inefficiencies occur. Any point along a production possibility frontier indicates optimum efficiency, i.e. maximum possible production using all available resources. Movements away from the origin indicate economic growth and higher levels of potential wealth.

Quickie ✔

Why might greater spending on capital goods lead to greater long-term production of consumption goods?

Puzzler *(but only for the hot shot mathematicians)*

Why do you think production possibility frontiers are usually drawn as curves rather than straight lines?

Trade and welfare

Trade and welfare are two more key economic concepts useful in helping to develop an understanding of economics. Trade refers to the exchange of goods and services. Welfare is used to indicate how well off a particular society might be.

A simple model of economic development

The growth of economies can be seen to involve four important developments:

- the production of surpluses
- growth of trade
- specialisation
- division of labour.

Surpluses

The development of western and other civilisations is closely linked to the development of trade. Much economic activity in the past is described as subsistence, whereby small groups within societies attempted to produce sufficient food and basic products to survive through their own labour. The survival of many subsistence economies was fraught with difficulties. Poor harvests could mean that there would not be enough food. Natural disasters could wipe out possessions and shelter. Many people still live like this and famine and natural disaster remain commonplace.

Trade

Making connections

Why were Henry Ford and Frederick Taylor so important?

Subsistence economies that became more successful were able to produce more food and goods than needed for immediate survival. They were able to store unused produce, perhaps to provide an insurance against unforeseen disasters. These surpluses could also be traded with other groups producing surpluses of their own.

Trade enabled greater prosperity and higher standards of living. Early trade was probably by barter in which one group of people with a surplus of fish, for example, would swap with another group able to produce, say, more grain. Barter is hardly a convenient form of trade so shells and other small precious items were used as early forms of money, and by 3000 years ago coins were being used as we use them today.

Research task

What is the oldest reference you can find to markets?

The combination of surpluses, money and growing trade provided the foundations for the development of markets – places at which trade could take place – which in turn provided a further stimulus for more economic growth and development.

Specialisation

Trade meant that an individual group no longer needed to attempt to supply all its own requirements. Different natural conditions might mean that others would be better at producing different commodities. Some could specialise in products they were best or most efficient at producing. Concentration on producing particular goods would increase overall production, leading to even more trade, the development of larger surpluses and higher standards of living.

The significance of specialisation is that if opportunity costs differ, and if groups and countries concentrate on producing those goods and services at which they are relatively more efficient, then everyone can become better off. This will only be true if trade is undertaken fairly.

Division of labour

Within societies, different tasks were increasingly delegated to particular individuals and groups. Through this division of labour, people were able to improve their skills and increase productivity so that more was produced. In this way past empires and dynasties grew and developed. Those that were most successful were able to use their surpluses to finance buildings, public works, religious celebrations and the like. Anything that would make a society better off without making someone else worse off would be described by economists as 'contributing to the improvement of the economic welfare of a society' – known as welfare for short.

A brief history of time

These developments can be seen in the social and economic history of the UK. In medieval England, growing agricultural surpluses led to an expansion in trade in wool and other products. Developing trade was accompanied by the development of towns and the emergence of merchants, traders and bankers.

The Industrial Revolution intensified these changes, especially in terms of the organisation of production in factories where division of labour was applied. Trade – both national and international – grew, leading to further economic growth and the creation of more wealth.

Today we are said to live in a global economy in which specialisation and the division of labour are played out on a worldwide scale. Companies such as Honda, Unilever and Benetton produce and market all over the world. International trade is even more important, and production tends to move to where it is cheapest. These processes by which we have all been drawn into a worldwide market of production and consumption are usually referred to as **globalisation.**

Quickie
Where would we be without money?

Definitions

Absolute advantage – A country is said to have an absolute advantage in the production of a good or service if it can produce it more cheaply than any competitor.

Comparative advantage – A country has a comparative advantage if it produces a good or service at a lower opportunity cost than any competitor.

Key concept

Comparative advantage – if opportunity costs differ and groups concentrate on producing goods and services at which they are more efficient, then everyone can become better off. This will only happen, however, if trade is undertaken fairly. This principle is developed in the A2 part of this course.

Hot potato

Is globalisation a good thing?

Demand

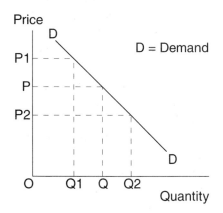

Figure 1 Changing prices

Demand has a very precise meaning in economics. It refers to how much of a product or service consumers are prepared to buy. Demand theory is based on a simple generalisation about customer behaviour. If CDs become more expensive, sales are likely to fall. But if they become cheaper, sales will probably rise. In other words, if the price of something rises, consumers are less likely to buy it, whereas falling prices lead to higher demand. This is illustrated in Figure 1.

The quantity demanded of a product or service is measured along the horizontal axis and its price on the vertical. The curve **DD** slopes downwards from left to right, showing that as the price lowers, demand rises. Thus, if the price is set at **P**, the demand will be at **Q**. If the price is increased to **P1**, the demand will fall to **Q1**. On the other hand, if the price falls to **P2**, the demand will rise to **Q2**. Any change in the price of a good will lead to a movement up or down the demand curve.

Changes in demand

Many factors are likely to have a potential influence on the demand for a product or service. Economists group these other key variables under the following headings.

- The price of other goods and services.
- Consumer income.
- Consumer taste.

Any change in these variables will lead to a shift in the demand curve.

The price of other goods and services

Clearly the decision to buy or not to buy something is not made simply on the basis of its price. Our decision to buy a particular product is usually informed by reference to prices of similar products. Goods such as Ford Fiestas and Renault Clios, which could be seen as alternatives for each other, are called substitutes. Some products or services, like shampoo and conditioner, are often used together. They are called complements.

Consumer income

Obviously the level of our income will have a powerful effect on our demand. The more we earn, the more we can buy, and vice versa. To be more precise, economists use the term **disposable income** to describe the amount of money available for spending after income tax has been deducted.

Goods for which demand increases boradly in line with incomes are classified as normal goods. Those products, e.g. travel on luxury liners, where demand rises proportionally more than income are known as **luxury goods**.

Other products are classified as **inferior goods**, in the sense that as consumer incomes rise, demand for certain products falls, and vice versa. Terraced houses in some areas of northern cities can be described in this way. As owners of such houses become better off, they are more likely to purchase more expensive **substitutes**.

Goods for which demand increases broadly in line with income are classified as normal goods.

Consumer taste

This term is used by economists to describe a whole range of other influences on demand. At one level we all like and dislike different things and these personal preferences are likely to affect what we buy. These individual differences are hard for economists to model but it is easier to identify broad trends and changes in tastes. Advertisers in particular try to change our tastes in order to increase the demand for particular products or services.

What if key variables change?

The demand curve introduced in Figure 1 is a graphical model that can be used to show the effects of changes in the three key variables. If the price of Renault Clios were to fall and the prices of other similar cars were to stay the same, the demand for Fiestas would fall. This is shown in Figure 2 by a shift in the demand to the left. If the opposite were to happen, the curve should shift to the right.

If goods are complements, a rise in the price of one will lead to a fall in demand for the other good.

Rising incomes will lead to an increase in demand for, say, foreign holidays and would also be shown by a shift in the demand curve to the right. If the good is considered inferior, then demand will fall as shown by a shift to the left.

Finally, changes in tastes can be treated in a similar way. The demand for goods that become more fashionable will shift to the right, whereas a leftward shift would show that something is no longer fashionable.

Quickie ✔

Which way will the demand curve for Mars Bars move if:
(a) the price of Twix is reduced
(b) child benefit is raised
(c) eating chocolate is proved to reduce your intelligence
(d) Tesco launches a two-for-the-price-of-one Mars Bar offer?

Puzzler *(this is hard!)*

What do you think economists are talking about when they refer to the differences between a 'shift' and a 'movement' along a demand curve?

Thinking like an economist

Model building is part of the essential toolkit of economists. Demand and supply analysis is one of the most simple and powerful models. Models are created in order to simplify sets of complex relationships. Section 1.5 is about the demand bit of demand and supply analysis. Following sections will help you to build an understanding of how to use demand and supply to identify what might be happening in marketplaces. Just remember, the value of any model will be determined by how well it replicates reality and how it can be used to predict what might happen if changes take place.

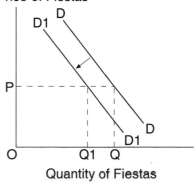

Figure 2 Demand shifts

Supply

1.6

Ceteris paribus

This piece of Latin means 'other things being equal'. Economists use this as a device for analysing complex situations when lots of things happen at once. It would be difficult to work out what would happen to coffee supply if there were a frost in Brazil, revolution in Columbia, collapse in tea prices and changes in demand in different countries. To make this kind of situation more manageable, economists freeze all but the variables they want to analyse. To make sure everyone knows what's going on, they use the phrase '*ceteris paribus*'.

Definition

A **supply curve** shows the likely relationship between the price of a good or service and the quantity supplied. The curve **SS** usually slopes upwards from left to right showing that as price rises supply is also likely to rise, whereas if price falls supply is likely to fall.

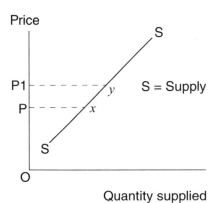

Figure 1 A typical supply curve

upply refers to the willingness and ability of a producer to supply a good or service. A typical supply curve is illustrated in Figure 1. It slopes upwards from left to right showing that as the price of a good or service rises, suppliers are likely to want to produce and supply more of that good or service. Economists consider price to be the most important variable affecting supply, but they also recognise that supply will be affected by four other factors:

- costs
- technology
- relative profitability
- business objectives.

Price and supply

Supply refers to the willingness and ability to supply goods to a market and, as with demand, price is considered to be the most important variable. *Ceteris paribus* (if everything were to remain the same), if the price of a good or service rises, it will become more profitable to sell that good or service. If there are greater potential profits, it is reasonable to expect that producers will wish to produce more. Therefore it is argued that a rise in price will lead to an increase in supply. This is illustrated in Figure 1 by the movement along the curve from *x* to *y*. The converse (opposite) of this is also true. If prices fall, supply should also fall.

Changes in supply

The **supply curve** will shift if any of the following factors change.

Costs of production

Costs refer to all payments that have to be made in order to produce a good. *Ceteris paribus*, a rise in costs will lead to a fall in profits and the incentive to make a particular product or service will drop. Figure 2 illustrates how this will lead to a shift in supply to the left (from **S** to **S1**), showing that at all possible prices less will be supplied. The reverse argument applies – if costs fall, potential profits rise and supply will rise shown by a shift in the supply curve to the right, as illustrated in Figure 3.

Changes in technology

Technology, in the sense of how we produce goods or provide services, is changing all the time. Improvements in the way in which things are made or how services are provided can have a major impact on supply. Car producers have reduced both production and running costs by using plastic components rather than metal. Improvements in technology are often associated with reductions in the cost of production and they can be illustrated in a similar way. The adoption of better and cheaper ways of making something will shift the supply curve downward to the right (as Figure 3 shows), because the same quantity of goods can be supplied at less cost. On the other hand, the use of more complex or difficult technologies will shift a supply curve to the left (as shown in Figure 2).

Relative profitability

Many firms have some choice in what they actually produce. Farmers, for example, decide which crops to grow. This choice is likely to be governed by the relative profitability of producing different goods or services. If Tesco can negotiate a better deal with the suppliers of Whiskas cat food rather than Felix, it may be inclined to supply more Whiskas and less Felix. Not all business have such easy choices as changing what you produce or sell may take time, but the general rule is that if supplying an alternative product becomes more profitable, the supply of the good in question will fall, as shown in Figure 2. On the other hand, if the supply of an alternative becomes less profitable there could be shift to the right of the original product showing an increase in supply, as illustrated in Figure 3.

Business objectives

So far we have assumed that businesses will all respond in similar ways to changes in factors affecting their supply of a good or service. Obviously no two businesses are the same. As will be discussed later, some businesses are interested in quick profits at all costs while others might place greater emphasis on ethical considerations. Business decision-makers don't necessarily respond immediately to small changes in price. In this case rising prices might not lead to increased output, or improvements in technology might allow the same level of profit in return for working less hard. How individual businesses work and make decisions will affect supply, and this makes it harder for economists to make simple generalisations about supply.

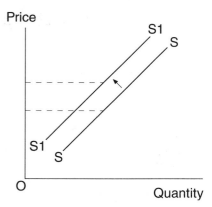

Figure 2 A rise in the cost of production

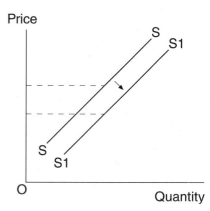

Figure 3 A fall in the cost of production

Quickie

Which way will the supply curve for Mars Bars move if:
(a) there is a severe frost in Ghana
(b) producing chocolate truffles becomes more profitable
(c) an ethical chocolate-producing company (e.g. Fairtrade) mounts a successful advertising campaign
(d) Mars Bars are shown to improve energy levels?

Puzzler (this is hard, but you have done it before!)

What do you think economists mean when they talk about the differences between a shift and a movement along a supply curve?

Elasticity

Elasticity is a key economics concept that comes up time and time again in different contexts. This is probably the first time you have come across this concept and it will pay to take some time to make sure your understanding is secure.

Price elasticity of demand

Basic economics indicates that if the price of a good or service changes, the demand will change. An increase in price is likely to result in a fall in demand, whereas a cut in price is likely to lead to an increase in quantity demanded. **Price elasticity of demand** is a way of measuring how much demand changes in response to change in price. Price elasticity can be analysed in three ways – by diagram, in words and by simple algebra.

Diagrammatical representation

Figures 1 (a) and (b) illustrate two very different responses in demand to identical reductions in price.

In the case of Figure 1(a), a cut of around 10 per cent in house prices from P to P1 leads to a rise in demand of about 50 per cent. In Figure 1(b) a larger price cut causes a much smaller rise in demand – about 5 per cent. The demand in Figure 1(a) is very responsive to changes in price, whereas in Figure 1(b) demand is much less responsive. Given the use of the same axis, the slope of the demand curve will indicate the degree of responsiveness to changes in price.

Another aspect shown most effectively by diagrams is to compare the revenue spent before and after the change. Revenue is simply price *x* quantity. In the first diagram, revenue rises and in the second it falls. This has massive implications for businesses selecting an appropriate pricing policy.

Words

Using words to describe the differences between the two diagrams involves some specialist terminology. If the demand for a good or service is very responsive to changes in price, then the demand is said to be relatively **elastic**. If the demand is relatively unresponsive to change, then the demand is described as relatively **inelastic**.

The formula

Using the formula for price elasticity of demand is a much more precise and mathematical way of dealing with the relationship between changes in price and changes in demand. The formula is:

$$\text{Price elasticity of demand (PED)} = \frac{\text{percentage change in quantity demanded}}{\text{percentage change in price}}$$

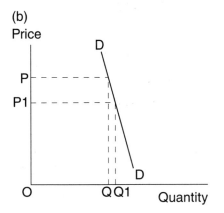

Figure 1 (a,b) Different responses in demand

So a price fall of 10 per cent accompanied by a demand increase of 50 per cent can be represented in the equation as follows:

$$PED = \frac{+50}{-10} = -5$$

Alternatively, if the price cut of 10 per cent prompted an increase in demand of 5 per cent, solving the same equation would give the following result:

$$PED = \frac{+5}{-10} = -0.5$$

These answers or values are called **co-efficients** and they give an instant insight into the responsiveness of demand for a product to a change in price. Any value, ignoring the + or – sign, which is less than 1, e.g. 0.6 or 0.2, indicates that demand for the product is not very responsive to changes in price. To be more precise, the percentage change in the price of the product will result in a smaller proportional change in quantity demanded.

On the other hand, a value that is larger than 1, e.g. 2.5 or 6, represents a demand that is very responsive to a change in price. The percentage change in quantity demanded for such a product will exceed the percentage change in price. Economists would describe this kind of demand response to be relatively elastic.

It may sound fussy, but never forget to include the plus or minus sign before the co-efficient. In the majority of cases this will be a minus.

Why elasticities differ

Economists consider that four factors have the greatest impact in determining the price elasticity of demand for a good or service.

- **Substitutes** – the demand for one brand of crisps will be more elastic if there are lots of similar brands on the market.
- **Disposable income** – the cheaper a good, the less sensitive it will make most buyers to price changes.
- **Consumer knowledge** – if customers don't know what substitutes are available or what they cost, demand is likely to be more inelastic.
- **Time** – it may take customers some time to adjust to changes in price; this would make price elasticity of demand more inelastic in the short run.

Quickies

- When will cutting the price of a good or service raise revenue?
- When can the same objective be achieved by raising prices?
- Why do UK governments often raise taxes on tobacco?

Puzzler

Why is the co-efficient for price elasticity of demand almost always a minus figure? What if it were a positive value?

Hot potato

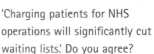

'Charging patients for NHS operations will significantly cut waiting lists.' Do you agree?

Making connections

What is the link between substitutes and competition?

Exam hint

Remember
Elasticity = elastic = stretches out = very responsive
Inelasticity = doesn't stretch = not very responsive

Other demand elasticities

1.8

At this stage in your studies you need to understand two other ways in which the concept of elasticity is used to help analyse different aspects of markets. They are:

- income elasticity of demand
- cross elasticity of demand.

Income elasticity of demand

Income elasticity of demand measures the responsiveness of the demand for a product to changes in incomes. It is represented by a formula or equation. In this case:

$$\text{Income elasticity of demand} = \frac{\text{percentage change in quantity demanded}}{\text{percentage change in income}}$$

Note: only the bottom of the equation changes with the different demand elasticities.

If the government were to decide to cut income taxes, then all those in work would have higher disposable incomes. Having more to spend might change people's spending patterns, especially if becoming better off makes it possible for them to afford what might have previously been considered a luxury item. Increasing incomes over the last 30 years, for example, have led to an even bigger proportionate increase in the demand for foreign holidays. This might mean that a 10 per cent rise in incomes could lead to a 30 per cent increase in the demand for foreign holidays. Therefore the income elasticity of demand for foreign holidays would be $\frac{+30}{+10}$ = +3. Goods such as these, for which there is positive income elasticity of demand, are called **superior goods, or luxury goods**.

On the other hand, rising incomes have also been associated with a fall in demand for traditional British seaside holidays. Therefore, the same increase in income of 10 per cent might be associated with a 40 per cent fall in demand for some English seaside towns. The income elasticity in this case would be $\frac{-40}{+10}$ = −4. The **co-efficient** for income elasticity of demand would in this case be negative. These would be described as **inferior goods**.

Cross elasticity of demand

As indicated in section 1.5, it is often helpful to categorise goods as being either **substitutes** or **complements**. These can be analysed using the concept of cross elasticity of demand, which is used to measure the responsiveness of demand for one good in relation to a change in the price of another.

Substitutes

Many people might regard peaches and nectarines as being close substitutes for each other. In this case an increase in the price of peaches may lead to an increase in the demand for nectarines. The formula used to work out the co-efficient of cross elasticity of demand is similar to those used earlier:

Cross elasticity of demand of good x
in relation to a change in the price of good $y =$

$$\frac{\text{percentage change in quantity demanded of good } x}{\text{percentage change in the price of good } y}$$

Therefore, if a 50 per cent increase in the price of peaches resulted in a 40 per cent rise in demand for nectarines, the formula would be:

$$\frac{+40}{+50} = +0.9$$

The value of the co-efficient will always be positive if you are considering two goods that are substitutes for each other.

The size of the co-efficient indicates how substitutable the two products are for one another. If there were little brand loyalty and a high degree of customer knowledge, the value of the co-efficient would be much larger.

Complements

If two sets of goods are complements, the co-efficient of the cross elasticity of demand of one good in respect of a change in the price of another will always be negative. For example, a fall in the mortgage rate is likely to lead to an increase in the demand for homes. In this case, a price cut of one good might lead to an increase in demand for a complement. Thus, a cut in interest rates of 1 per cent may lead to a 10 per cent increase in demand for houses giving a value of –10. The relatively large negative figure would indicate that the demand for houses is very sensitive to changes in the mortgage interest rates. If two goods are complements their co-efficient for their cross elasticities will always be negative and, as with all the other uses of elasticity, the smaller the value the less responsive the relationship, and vice versa.

Hot potato

Why is branding so important in marketing?

Exam hint

Small value to elasticity co-efficient = weak relationship.
Large value = strong relationship.
Negative value = inverse relationship.

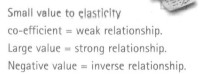

Quickie ✓

What do the following co-efficients indicate?
- yed   =   –2
- xed   =   +0.5
- yxed   =   –5

1.9 Elasticity of supply

The responsiveness of supply to changes in price is measured using the concept of elasticity of supply. As with other applications of this concept, economists use written, graphical and algebraic treatments.

Words

If it is easy and quick for a producer to change the output of a good or service in response to changes in price, then the supply of that good is described as relatively elastic. Alternatively, if it is difficult and time consuming to change output in response to price changes, then supply is relatively inelastic.

Graphs

Graphical analysis can quickly be used to illustrate supply elasticity. Figure 1(a) illustrates inelastic supply and Figure 1(b) elastic supply.

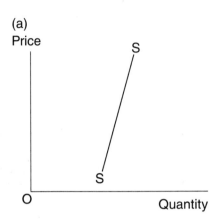

(a)

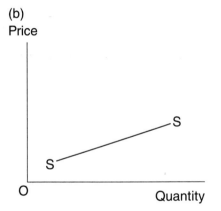

(b)

Figure 1 (a) Relatively inelastic supply
(b) Relatively elastic supply

The formula

The formula for working out the co-efficient is very similar to that relating to price elasticity of demand. It is:

$$\text{Elasticity of supply} = \frac{\%\ \text{change in quantity supplied}}{\%\ \text{change in price}}$$

Thus, if the price of cars rises by 10 per cent and car producers struggle hard to raise output, increasing supply by 2 per cent, the co-efficient would be + 0.2. If, on the other hand manufacturers have large stocks of unsold cars and can change output quickly in response to a price rise, the co-efficient is likely to be larger than 1. It is very unlikely for a negative co-efficient to occur, as this would mean that producers expand production in response to a fall in price or cut output in response to a rise in price.

The opposite analysis also applies. Falling prices are associated with a decrease in willingness to produce and supply. Some producers are able to adjust quickly to falling prices, while others will find it harder to do.

Factors affecting the elasticity of supply

If prices rise, producers are likely to want to respond by increasing production and this could be achieved by undertaking a programme of measures. The elasticity of supply of any product or service is likely to depend on the following factors.

- Availability of stocks, and raw materials. (If there are stocks of finished goods, components and other materials it will be relatively easy to expand production and sales. Conversely, expansion could be slowed by the unavailability of one small component.)
- Unused productive capacity. (If existing factories and production lines are not being used all the time, supply is likely to be more elastic.)
- Availability of imports. (Many industries are global and companies can switch supplies from shrinking markets to those that are growing.)
- Availability of suitably trained labour. (The difficulty and extra costs of attracting skilled workers will limit the responsiveness of producers in meeting increases in demand.)

The significance of these factors can be viewed in a different way by using the concept of 'time' – the supply of most products and services is likely to become more elastic over a longer timescale. Changes in elasticity of supply over time are shown in Figure 2. **S** represents the elasticity of supply in a very short **timescale** as unused stocks of materials and under-utilised labour are used, S1 for a longer period in which existing productive capacity can be brought into production, and S2 over an even longer period to allow for the acquisition of new plant and machinery along with the training of new workers.

The significance of technological change

Technological change refers to changes in the way in which goods and services are actually produced. Over the last two decades, tremendous advances have been made in communications technology. We all know about the importance of IT in our lives but there have been similar, if less spectacular, advances in air and sea transport. These developments have been paralleled by the growth of transnational corporations – many of which have more economic power than most nations. The cumulative effect of these changes is often referred to as globalisation. It is now possible for production and sales to be organised on a global scale, which means that the supply of many products and services has become more and more elastic. As will be shown in later sections of this book, globalisation has a major effect on how economies and economists work.

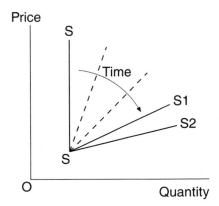

Figure 2 Elasticity of supply changing over time

Quickies

- What factors are likely to affect the elasticity of supply in the following markets?
(a) Wheat production.
(b) Electrical generation.
(c) Tee-shirt manufacture.
- Which supply is likely to be most responsive to changes in demand/price?

Markets exist wherever those who demand products or services meet those who supply goods or services. Many different kinds of markets exist. The earliest markets moved around the country and were often celebrated as fairs and special events where all kinds of resources were traded. Some were devoted to selling surplus production at harvest time, while others involved selling labour to the highest bidders. Cattle markets retain some of the features of these earlier trading events. Towns and city centres now take on many of the functions of traditional markets, and the sellers of products and services use a wide variety of strategies to appeal to consumers. There are many other forms of market including:

- classified advertisements
- the stock market
- wholesale markets
- futures market
- auctions
- flea markets
- black markets
- grey markets
- the Internet.

This list could easily be extended, but irrespective of the form and frequency of such markets they all involve:

- buyers
- sellers
- a means to reach a deal.

Putting demand and supply together

As demand curves and supply curves are drawn against the same axes, it is possible to superimpose one on top of another, as illustrated in Figure 3, which shows the market for new houses.

The demand for new houses slopes downward to the right. It is relatively inelastic, as there are not many close substitutes. Supply slopes upward to the right. This is also relatively inelastic for the new houses as it is not always easy for producers to quickly change output in response to changes in demand and price.

The point x, where the supply and demand curves cross, shows the price at which demand and supply are equal. In this example, the average price of a new house coming on the market will be £85,000 and 100 houses would be

Figure 1 The stock exchange

Figure 2 A flea market – another type of market

sold each month. This is called the **equilibrium** price and in a free market this will be established automatically. If for some reason the price were to rise, supply would be greater than demand. The producers of new houses would be attempting to sell more than could be sold.

This **excess supply** of 30 homes would mean that some houses were being made but not sold. Stocks of unwanted houses would build up and sellers would be tempted to cut prices. Falling prices would make new houses more attractive to some consumers, while some builders may find house building less attractive because of the potential lower profit, and seek alternative building contracts. Demand would then rise as supply fell. According to price theory, this process would stop when the equilibrium price was reached. This pincer movement to the establishment of an equilibrium is shown by the two movements *a* and *b* along the demand and supply curves. This process by which markets are brought into equilibrium is called **market clearing**.

The same logical analysis can be applied to a situation in which new houses are being sold for less than £85,000. In this case, demand would be **greater** than supply. Excess demand would apply and some prospective house buyers would be forced to go without. New houses coming onto the market would be snapped up quickly, and enterprising estate agents might well attempt to take advantage of shortages of new houses by raising their prices. This process would set a similar pincer movement in operation. Rising prices would put off some potential house buyers but would also make house production more attractive. Demand would fall and supply would rise until equilibrium reached at £85,000.

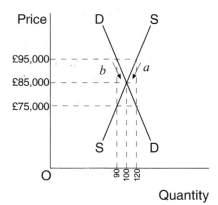

Figure 3 The market for new houses

Summary

The key point is that as long as demand curves slope downwards to the right and supply curves slope upwards to the right, and as long as they both cross, there will be only one equilibrium – and that is the price where demand is equal to supply. In other words, both buyers and sellers can make a deal.

Web link

For more information on markets and demand, visit www.heinemann.co.uk/hotlinks and type in express code 0829P.

Quickies ✔

- How far back in time do markets go?
- Are markets a good idea?
- How many different kinds of market can you list? Make a note of them.

Markets and changes in supply

Changes in supply can be considered in the context of the market for organically grown carrots. In this case, supply will change if any of the following happen:

- production costs change
- technology changes
- there are changes in the objectives of producers.

The market for organic carrots

In this market there will be a considerable number of producers, both in this country and abroad. Individually, they will have much less influence over the price charged for their product. However, as shown in Figure 1, it is reasonable to assume that the supply of organic carrots is likely to slope upwards from left to right as with **S**. This shows a greater willingness to produce if prices are high and vice versa. The demand curve for organic carrots is likely to be relatively inelastic and this is shown by the steep gradient of **DD**. In this market, demand and supply are equal at price **P**, leading to sales of **Q**.

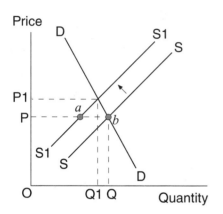

Figure 1 Effects of increased costs faced by organic carrot producers

Increasing costs of production

Organic producers face additional costs in order to assure buyers that their produce is really organic. Thus the Soil Association operates a certification scheme to guarantee the organic origins of products. If it were to increase its registration fees, organic carrot producers would be faced with an increase in costs. This is shown in Figure 1 by the leftward and upward shift in supply to **S1**.

If the price were to remain at **P** per kilo, demand will now exceed supply by *a b*. Excess demand means that some potential buyers might have to go without; enterprising greengrocers might raise their prices. The price is likely to rise until a new equilibrium is reached. In this case, demand will be equal to the reduced supply at **P1** per kilo, and sales will fall from **Q** to **Q1**.

Hot potato

'The case for organic food production in the UK is overwhelming.' Do you agree?

Thinking like an economist

When you get used to using demand and supply analysis to predict what will happen if a key variable changes, you will soon realise that it is possible to argue different outcomes from the same starting point. Make sure your order of events is logical and that each step in your reasoning is clear.

Improvements in technology

Alternatively, as Figure 2 illustrates, a technological improvement could be made in the production process that reduces costs of supply. Potential profits would be higher. Production would be more attractive and the supply curve would shift downwards to the right. If the old price were maintained, disequilibrium would arise in which supply was greater than demand (at Q2). Prices would fall until a new equilibrium were established showing both a lower price (P1) and higher sales (Q1). The increase in supply from SS to S1S1 leads to low prices and increased sales.

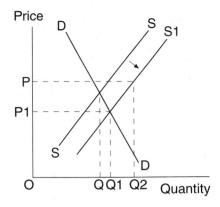

Figure 2 Effects of technological improvements on the organic carrot market

Objectives of producers

An increasing number of farmers are turning away from using inorganic fertilisers, herbicides and pesticides and may prefer to adopt organic techniques for ethical reasons. This trend is likely to lead to an increase in the supply of organic products, as shown in Figure 2. The long-term effect of these trends is that the supply and sales of organic carrots and other products should increase and prices should fall.

The importance of elasticity

The significance of elasticity of demand is illustrated in Figure 3 (a,b). In the first diagram, demand is highly inelastic, whereas the second shows a highly elastic demand. The same change in supply in both markets will have very different effects on both price and sales.

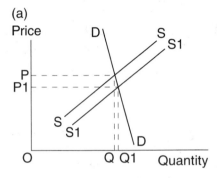

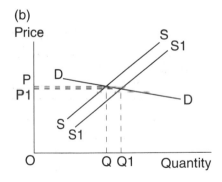

Figure 3 (a) Inelastic and (b) elastic demand

Quickie

How might the price and sales of hot chocolate in the UK be affected by:

(a) easier access for African producers to European markets

(b) a new outbreak of foot and mouth disease in the UK

(c) more hurricanes in the West Indies

(d) lower tea prices?

Factor markets

1.12

The market system includes a whole series of markets for the factors of production – land, labour, capital and enterprise. Collectively, these are called factor markets. They play a crucial role in ensuring that customers get those goods and services they wish to purchase. Although economists consider that there are special features of these markets, demand and supply analysis is used to model the behaviour of those working in factor markets.

Demand for factors

Factors of production are, in many senses, like any other product that is traded in the marketplace. They have a price. The price of labour, for example, is the wage or salary that has to paid. Rent is the return earned by the owners of land. Profit is a reward for enterprise and interest, or dividends can be seen as the price paid to the owners of money or capital. If a factor of production, other things being equal, is expensive then the demand is likely to be low. If, on the other hand, they are cheap, demand will be high. Therefore, the demand for building land will be lower as it becomes more expensive. In other words, the demand for factors is likely to slope downwards from left to right as shown in Figure 1.

Figure 1 The supply of workers for lower paying jobs

Supply of factors

Similar analysis can be applied to the supply of factors. If it is assumed that the owners of factors of production are materialistic (they want to make as good a financial return as possible from the factors that they own), then the supply of land, labour, capital or enterprise, can be treated in much the same way as the supply of any commodity. The supply of workers to higher-paying jobs is likely to be higher than that to similar jobs paying lower wages. Alternatively, if wages are low then the supply is likely to be low. This means that a supply curve for any factor will slope upwards to the right as illustrated by S in Figure 1.

Making connections

Is the demand for labour constant throughout the year?

Thinking like an economist

Remember, the demand for factors is derived from the demand for a final product or service, and the supply of factors in some cases can be fixed or immobile.

Factor market equilibrium

This is illustrated in Figure 1. Although this looks like any other demand and supply diagram, the axes measure different variables. If the market for shop workers in Cheltenham is being modelled, wages are represented on the vertical axis and numbers employed on the horizontal. The equilibrium wage rate is given as £6 per hour, at which the demand for shop workers is matched by the supply at Q. Any change in demand and supply will lead to the establishment of a new equilibrium.

Derived demand

Final goods like cars or houses are demanded for what they are. Factors are demanded not for what they are but because they are required to produce something else. Their demand is said to be 'derived'. This means that the nature of the demand for the final product will have a direct impact on the demand for the factors required to produce that product. Therefore, the demand for pesticide-free land will increase as a result of the increase in demand for organic foodstuffs, while the demand for meat-processing equipment falls as a result of the fall in demand for meat products. Premier division footballers command enormous salaries because they contribute to the success and earnings of top clubs.

Although the demand curve for a factor of production looks like any other demand curve, its gradient and position will be heavily influenced by the demand for the final product. If the demand for that final product is highly price elastic then it is likely that the demand for factors to make that product will also be relatively elastic. Similarly, if the demand for the final product is relatively inelastic, use is likely to be more stable. It follows that if there is a sudden surge in demand for Thai food, there will be a surge in demand for Thai chefs, and they are likely to be paid more than those producing different food products.

Factor immobility

The supply of factors is also special in some ways. In the case of labour markets, we are considering people and it may not be appropriate to treat people as commodities.

Moreover, people may not work solely for monetary reward. Some jobs are more attractive than others, irrespective of wages or salary levels. Some people are loath to leave some parts of the country for others, even though wages and salaries might be higher.

The use of others factors of production may be even less flexible because some may be fixed in supply. Thus, in the UK the amount of land for new housing developments tends to be fixed for a mixture of reasons. Land itself is finite. It can't be moved from one part of the country to another.

The mobility of labour or any other factor of production can be illustrated by the gradient of the supply curve (as in Figure 2 (a, b)). In the most extreme case (there is only one David Beckham), the supply curve will be vertical, indicating a fixed supply irrespective of the wage or return offered. On the other hand, the supply of Division 3 players is much more elastic.

> **Quickie**
>
> How far can the concepts of demand and supply be used to explain the differences in earning between successful bands and those who struggle to make ends meet?

Hot potato

Why do women get paid less than men?

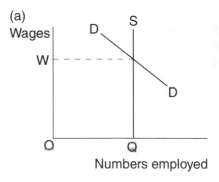

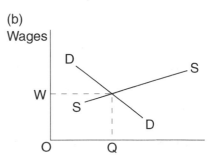

Figure 2 (a) The David Beckham supply curve
(b) The supply of Division 3 players

How the price mechanism works

Definition

The **price mechanism** refers to a complex set of relationships that, in theory, link consumers and their wants to suppliers and producers, who in turn buy factors of production to produce the goods in demand.

Knowing how individual markets work is a key step on the way to understanding how a whole market economy works. No market works in isolation from other markets. Changes in one market will lead to changes in others, which will have further effects. These chain reactions have a big impact on our lives. They can cause us to become richer or poorer. They have an impact upon the environment. They can change the way we see things. This complex set of interrelationships is called the **price mechanism**.

Local market interrelationships

The housing boom in the south-east of England in the late 1990s and early 2000s was caused by a major imbalance between the supply and demand for housing. Greater London contains a vast array of businesses, government departments and so on. Although there are many existing on low incomes, London also contains a disproportionate number of people earning high incomes. Houses are a superior good and have a high income elasticity of demand. Moreover, the demand for houses in London and the south-east is greater than in other parts of the country.

The supply of houses in the short run is relatively inelastic, resulting in relatively high house prices. In 2002, land prices continued to rise. The demand for workers with building skills rose, boosting the earning of bricklayers and other skilled trades. Estate agents found both sales and high profits easy to earn. The demand for all kinds of building materials escalated. Earnings of workers and the profits of the owners of such businesses also climbed.

Rising house prices in London forced some potential house buyers to look further afield, pushing up the demand for housing in the counties around London and causing similar chain reactions as increases in demand in one market rippled over into closely related markets. It would be possible to construct an ever-growing web of relationships and interrelationships as partially illustrated in Figure 1 below.

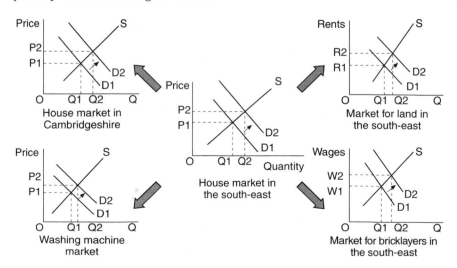

Figure 1 Part of the price mechanism

What has been described is only part of the picture. There are great pressures to turn farmland into new estates. Road congestion is getting worse and so on. It is easy to see how such ripples and waves would set off further reactions. It is also possible to visualise the rise in property prices in the south-east of England reaching out and affecting the whole local economy.

Thus, any local economy consists of thousands of interconnected markets, each with its own demand and supply curves shifting and adjusting to change after change. The key links between these individual markets are price changes.

- The rise in the price of houses is a signal to those who supply associated products like paint, nails, furnishings and washing machines, that they should consider increasing their supplies and raising their prices.
- Rising incomes in the building trade will act as a signal to attract more workers to move to the region and more young people to undertake training.
- Rising profits could also lead to increases in the share prices of leading building firms.
- The demand for water, electricity and other utilities will also rise.

National interrelationships

The tentacles of the price mechanism spread far and wide. The impact of the property boom was not confined to the south-east. Brick makers in Bedford, timber suppliers in Scotland and screw makers in Birmingham would all experience growing orders. Demand for their products would have risen alongside demand for labour and other resources. A whole series of demand curves would shift to the right, and prices and outputs rise.

Ever-growing congestion and rising land prices in the south-east would encourage some employers to re-locate to other parts of the country. Spreading business activity from London also affects motorways and rail links.

Global effects

The effects of the property boom also spread beyond the UK. Foreign suppliers of building materials, furnishings and the like enjoyed increased demand for their products. Workers from Ireland and southern European countries were attracted to Britain because of labour shortages, especially in the hotel and catering industries. The property boom spread to northern France and southern Ireland, as those in high-earning jobs in the UK spent part of their increased incomes on holiday and weekend homes.

Quickie

Make sure you understand each step in the mechanism outlined in this section by working out the effects of everyone wanting to have red hair.

1.14 Advantages of the price mechanism

Definitions

66 99

Remember, allocative efficiency refers to who gets what. An economy would be allocatively efficient if everybody received exactly those goods and services for which they were prepared to pay the market price.

Productive efficiency refers to producing goods and services at the lowest possible average cost.

Thinking like an economist

How accurately does the free market model describe how our economy actually works? Are consumers sovereign? Are firms compelled to be as efficient as possible?

This section considers the theoretical advantages of the price mechanism, and builds on earlier treatments of how individual markets work and interact with each other. The two great theoretical advantages are:

- consumer sovereignty
- productive efficiency.

Consumer sovereignty

This term is used to show that if the price mechanism were to work in the way described, there would be consumer sovreignty. It is argued that changes in consumer preferences will eventually determine which of the earth's scarce resources will be used and to what end. Therefore, if customers want to consume more organic products, they will be prepared to pay more for them than non-organics, retailers will respond by stocking more organics and these changes will ripple through the price mechanism resulting in some farmers switching to organic methods. At the same time, demand for pesticides and other products associated with non-organic production methods will fall. This should eventually result in the reduction in number and size of buisnesses who supply pesticides and so on.

The principle of consumer sovereignty relates to the central questions that economics is meant to answer. What gets produced? How is it produced? Who gets what is produced? If the price mechanism is allowed to work freely, it is argued that we actually end up using resources to reflect exactly customer preferences.

Productive efficiency

This is a bit more complicated and will repay careful reading. In the price mechanism it is assumed that just as there are many consumers, there are many producers who will be forced by market pressures to produce outputs at which costs of production are minimised. The reasons for this have been implicit in how the price mechanism has been described earlier and can be represented as follows.

Assume one firm operating in one industry discovers a new, more efficient way of making what it produces, and follow the process of what then happens as a consequence.

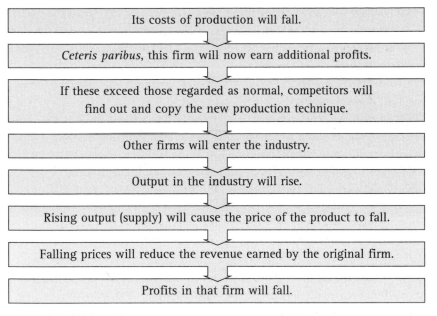

| Its costs of production will fall. |
| Ceteris paribus, this firm will now earn additional profits. |
| If these exceed those regarded as normal, competitors will find out and copy the new production technique. |
| Other firms will enter the industry. |
| Output in the industry will rise. |
| Rising output (supply) will cause the price of the product to fall. |
| Falling prices will reduce the revenue earned by the original firm. |
| Profits in that firm will fall. |

On the other hand, if the demand for a particular product or service falls the following will happen:

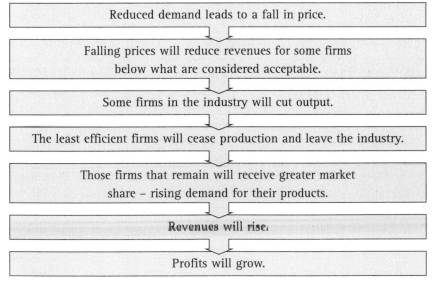

| Reduced demand leads to a fall in price. |
| Falling prices will reduce revenues for some firms below what are considered acceptable. |
| Some firms in the industry will cut output. |
| The least efficient firms will cease production and leave the industry. |
| Those firms that remain will receive greater market share – rising demand for their products. |
| Revenues will rise. |
| Profits will grow. |

In short, the forces of competition are such that the efficiency and cost-cutting of one firm will be copied by competitors, and any contraction in demand will be accompanied by the disappearance of the least efficient producers. This is a continuing process that should result in ever-growing efficiencies in those markets that are truly competitive.

Summary

The price mechanism is meant to achieve two important outcomes: we get what we want, at the lowest possible price – not bad – but this is only half the story, as the following section indicates.

Figure 1 Adam Smith, 5 June 1723 – 17 July 1790

Adam Smith was a Scottish political economist and philosopher. In 1776, he wrote *Wealth of Nations*, which has become a work of major importance in the world of economics.

'The uniform, constant and uninterrupted effort of every man to better his condition, the principle from which public and national, as well as private opulence is originally derived, is frequently powerful enough to maintain the natural progress of things toward improvement, in spite both of the extravagance of government, and of the greatest errors of administration.'

Adam Smith, *Wealth of Nations*

Research task

Find more information on Adam Smith.

Disadvantages of the price mechanism

There are four main criticisms of the price mechanism. They are linked to:

- equity
- realism
- factor immobility
- market failure.

The last of these, market failure, is such a big topic that it justifies the whole module of study which you will tackle after studying *Markets – how they work*. At this stage, all you need to know is that markets don't necessarily work in the way they are meant to. The other possible disadvantages include the following.

Equity

Does the price mechanism produce fair outcomes?

You should remember the distinction between wants and demand. Economists define demand as wants backed up by the ability to pay for what is demanded. But income and wealth are not equally distributed. For example, the developed countries in the world contain 25 per cent of world population, yet they consume 80 per cent of the world's resources. Is this fair? One-third of the world's population doesn't get enough to eat. Some would argue that this is a direct result of an over-reliance on the price mechanism to allocate the world's resources. Not all consumers are on an equal footing. Those with wealth and large incomes are able to consume disproportionate amounts of resources, while those with little wealth or income go without.

The unequal distribution of income in all societies can lead to most resources being used for the production of luxury goods for the well off. Such extremes are often clearly evident in many countries in the developing world, but they also exist in the UK. Thus, in this country there are persistent shortages of affordable housing, and in its most extreme form a significant minority of people are homeless.

Realism

Like demand and supply, the price mechanism can be seen as a model that is meant to accurately reflect the world as we know it. Model building involves making assumptions and approximations. If these are unsound, the use and value of any model is limited. Critics of the model of the price mechanism claim that it represents a gross oversimplification of how economic activity actually works. Two related criticisms are important.

- Implicit in the model is the notion of consumer rationality and perfect knowledge. But consumers might be ignorant and may act irrationally. They might not know what goods and services are available. They have

Making connections

What happens to consumer sovreignty if factors of production are not mobile?

Thinking like an economist

By now you should be getting used to how economists use models to understand complex relationships. Although the price mechanism is a great simplification of what really goes on, it is useful in helping to understand these complex processes. The fact that this model has weaknesses does not justify rejecting it out of hand.

little idea of the prices of substitutes. Millions of pounds are spent on advertising in order to influence and mould peoples' tastes.

- The model also assumes a greater level of competition between firms than may actually be the case. The price mechanism assumes that competition is open and vigorous. Some firms may have more power and influence than is taken account of in the model of the price mechanism. Moreover, it is assumed that there is freedom of entry and exit from all industries. In reality, both large and small companies often try to find ways of limiting competition and keeping new firms out. In some cases there may be no competition. **Monopolies** are so powerful that they, rather than consumers, can determine what is produced.

Definition

A **monopoly** exists when there is only one company or supplier within a particular industry.

Factor immobility

If the price mechanism is going to work effectively, factors of production need to be mobile in response to changes in price. In other words, if there is an increase in demand for plumbers in London, plumbers should move to the capital because relative pay rates will have increased. Similarly, more young people might consider plumbing a more attractive job. The assumption is that changes in wages or salaries are the most important factor determining what jobs people do. This assumption might be an oversimplification, and even if it were true, there might be other factors limiting the movement of plumbers or any other workers. In the example of London, the availability of affordable housing has been a major issue. Similarly, the free movement of entrepreneurial skills is likely to be constrained by various human and social factors.

Land and capital can be even less mobile. Some machinery can only be used for one purpose. Although land and its resources can be switched between uses, the physical amount of land is fixed.

Summary

In theory, the price mechanism predicts that freely operating markets ensure that goods are produced most efficiently and that consumers determine how resources are used. In practice, this model oversimplifies some very complex relationships, ignores the existence of monopoly and factor immobility, and could result in a set of outcomes that could be considered socially undesirable. For this reason, every economy in the world contains a mixture of the market system and different forms of market intervention – usually by governments. Such societies are said to have mixed economies. More about this in the next section.

Hot potato

The poor have no one to blame but themselves. Do you agree?

Quickie

Why haven't increases in nurses' salaries resulted in a significant increase in the number of trained nurses?

1.16 Command economies

The price mechanism and freely functioning markets are very closely associated to the growth and development of capitalism. Inequalities and exploitation associated with capitalism resulted in the establishment, often through revolution, of communist states. These embraced a totally different form of economic organisation in which the state played a key role in determining the 'what and how' of production and the 'to whom' of distribution. Countries such as the former Soviet Union were said to have **command economies**. These differed from the market systems modelled on the working of the price mechanism in the following ways:

- ownership of resources
- decision making
- distribution.

Research task

Choose one of the former Eastern European countries and find out how successful it has been in transforming from a command to a market economy.

Making connections

Rationing in the UK during the Second World War reduced rickets - why?

Ownership of resources

With a pure version of the free market economy, all resources are privately owned but in command economies, state and co-operative ownership of resources is much more common. In the former Czechoslovakia every business enterprise was owned by the state. In communist Hungary all but small businesses were state-owned.

Decision making

If all or most resources are owned by the state, it follows that most economic decisions are also taken by the state. The government would decide the what, the where and the how of production. This is relatively simple in terms of deciding about broad principles such as whether to produce more basic goods and fewer luxuries, but incredibly complex when it comes to deciding which of a broad range of consumer goods to produce. Decisions would be passed down to the managers and directors of different businesses, who would be given a series of production targets.

Distribution

If the price mechanism is allowed to work, the consumer is sovereign and customer preferences and the strength of individual demand determine who gets what in terms of production. With a command economy, this responsibility is taken over by the state. Thus, when the government took over many aspects of the UK economy in the Second World War, it issued ration books which ensured that limited supplies of food and other goods were equally shared between different people. This method can ensure a greater degree of equality than is likely using the price mechanism, but also creates the conditions for black markets to operate.

The rise and fall of command economies

Many command economies were replaced towards the end of the twentieth century by **mixed economies,** in which more importance was placed on the freely operating markets to allocate resources.

This process has been most evident in the former communist countries of Eastern Europe and the former Soviet Union. Although countries like Poland, Romania and Ukraine have changed in different ways, all have undergone changes to the ownership of resources, the infrastructure and openness to competition.

Switching to a market-based economy usually involves privatisation of significant sectors of the economy – the process by which ownership of resources is transferred from the state to private individuals. This can be done by giving loans to enable workers in small businesses to buy the companies where they work. Alternatively, shares can be issued or sold to ordinary people and/or foreign companies.

Figure 1 The UK chancellor, Gordon Brown, and the budget box - representative of a market-based economy at work

Infrastructure

In command economies, priority was usually given to investment in those projects that were considered to be politically important. Thus, the new Czech Republic has inherited a relatively effective system of public transport, reasonably equipped and run schools, and good levels of health care. However, there had been little incentive to modernise and improve key areas of economic infrastructure like roads and heavy industry. Improving and changing these has been difficult.

Competition

The lack of competition in command economies meant that workers had little or no motivation to be productive or quality conscious. There were few incentives for workers or managers to show initiative, and managers had little experience of dealing with the challenges and risks of the marketplace.

Summary

Most command economies have been abandoned, but the switch to a greater reliance on the price mechanism has been difficult and a combination of factors has meant that it is very difficult for countries who had command economies to compete with those who are more used to the pressures of market competition.

Puzzler

What features of the UK economy are characteristic of a command economy, and what features are characteristic of a free market economy?

Tax and spend

The UK is a mixed economy and around 40 per cent of output is determined by national and local government, not directly by market forces. Government expenditure has to be paid for. Hence if the government is going to spend, it also has to raise revenue in some way. The main way of doing this is through taxation. We pay what are called **direct taxes** like income tax, straight to the government. Other taxes like VAT and customs and excise duties on tobacco and petrol are called **indirect taxes**, because we only pay them if we purchase the goods or services on which they are levied. This section is concerned with indirect taxes and subsidies, as their application will have an effect on how markets and the price mechanism works.

Indirect taxes

Governments can have a distorting effect on freely operating markets if they decide to impose indirect taxes on particular goods or services. It is important to establish why governments decide to impose taxes. There are two main reasons:

- to raise revenue
- to cut the sales of a good or service that is judged harmful in some way.

The imposition of a tax adds to firms' costs and shifts the supply curve to the left, as shown in Figure 1. The vertical distance **ab** illustrates the amount of the tax.

Without a tax, the market equilibrium would settle at **x** giving a price of **P** and sales of **Q**. The effects of imposing a tax are to significantly push up the price paid by consumers to **P1**, but the effect on the amount sold drops only slightly to **Q1**.

The effects could be very different, as shown in Figure 2, which shows a large impact on sales but a small impact on demand.

It is important to note that the impact on price and sales will be determined by the slope of the demand curve. In Figure 1, the demand is relatively inelastic and the impact of the tax will be concentrated on the consumer. Such a tax will be a good revenue earner for the government but will have little impact on sales. Figure 2, where demand is relatively elastic, shows little impact on price, significant impact on sales and therefore only a small contribution to government revenue.

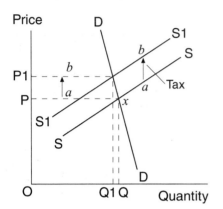

Figure 1 Effects of the imposition of an indirect tax: 1

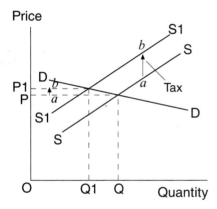

Figure 2 Effects of the imposition of an indirect tax: 2

Subsidies

Economists treat subsidies as reverse taxes on the basis that they are amounts paid to a producer by the government to provide a product or service. They may be paid to ensure that a particular service is provided that is considered to be socially useful – like some rural bus services – or they might be used to keep down the prices of particular goods or services. Their possible impact can be modelled in a similar way to that used for indirect taxes. The provision of a subsidy for a product for which the demand is relatively inelastic is shown in Figure 3 by a vertical shift downwards of the supply curve, leading to a significant fall in price from **P** to **P1** and small rise in sales from **Q** to **Q1**. Such a subsidy would be expensive to the government.

If, however, the demand for the product or service is relatively elastic, the imposition of a subsidy will have little effect on price and a relatively large impact on sales. A subsidy in these conditions would not be as expensive to the government. This is illustrated in Figure 4.

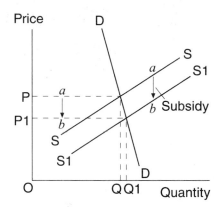

Figure 3 Effects of the imposition of a subsidy in a market with a relatively inelastic demand curve

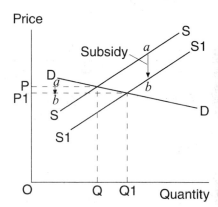

Figure 4 Effects of the imposition of a subsidy in a market with a relatively elastic demand curve

Quickie

'If the government wants to maximise the revenue it raises from indirect taxes, it should tax those goods for which there are many substitutes.' True or false?

Puzzler

Why does the UK government tax tobacco so heavily?

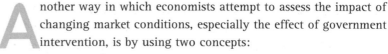

Consumer and producer surpluses

nother way in which economists attempt to assess the impact of changing market conditions, especially the effect of government intervention, is by using two concepts:

- consumer surplus
- producer surplus.

Consumer surplus

This concept uses graphical analysis to illustrate the benefits that customers gain from consuming a particular product or service. In Figure 1, **P** shows the equilibrium price, with the level of sales given at **Q**.

The horizontal axis can be taken to measure the number of customers for a particular product. The last customer is represented as **Q** and is prepared to pay the market price for the product, but all earlier customers would have been prepared to pay more. For instance, the **Q1** customer would have been prepared to pay more at **P1**, and the **Q2** customer would have been prepared to pay still more. The vertical distances between the market price and top section of the demand curve indicate how much more some customers would have been prepared to pay for the good or service. Taken together, the shaded area represents an additional benefit enjoyed by consumers of this product. This is referred to as consumer surplus.

Producer surplus

A similar analytical approach can be made to gains made by producers of a good or service. In Figure 2, producers receive **P** for their total output of **Q**, but all but the final producer would have been prepared to supply the good or service for less than the equilibrium price of **P**.

Definitions

Consumer surplus measures the benefits enjoyed by some consumers who are able to buy a good or service for less than they are prepared to pay.

Producer surplus measures the benefits enjoyed by some producers who would be prepared to supply a product or service for less than the market price.

Making connections

What happens to consumer and producer surpluses if demand and supply become more inelastic?

Exam hint

Diagrams like these, which can appear to be complicated, are a favourite for multiple-choice questions. Make sure you practise how surpluses are derived and sorting out which area is which.

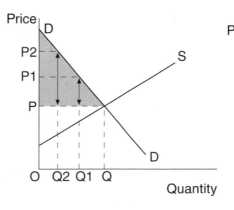

Figure 1 Consumer surplus

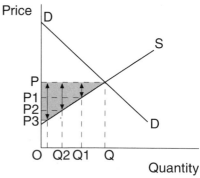

Figure 2 Producer surplus

Q1 producers were prepared to supply for **P1**, whereas **Q2** were prepared to accept even less at **P2**. The shaded area, below the price and above the left section of the supply curve, is said to represent producers' surplus. Figures 1 and 2 can be combined as shown in Figure 3 – area C showing consumer surplus and P the surplus for producers.

Assessing the impact of indirect taxation

This graphical analysis can be used to model the impact of the imposition of indirect taxation. As explained previously, this is shown by shifting the supply curve upwards by the amount of tax. Figure 4 shows that both consumer and producers lose out as both surpluses are reduced.

The converse of this is that cutting indirect taxes benefits both consumers and producers.

Assessing the impact of government subsidies

Similar analysis can be applied to the effect of government subsidy. As shown in Figure 5, any rightward shift in the supply curve will result in an increase in both customer and producer surpluses.

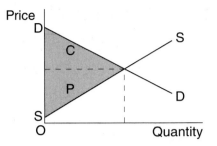

Figure 3 Consumer and producer surplus

> ### Quickie
>
> How might consumer and producer surplus be affected by:
> (a) reduction of barriers of entry in an industry
> (b) the establishment of a monopoly in an industry?

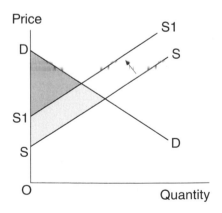

Figure 4 Falling surpluses

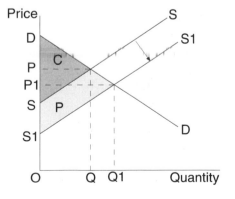

Figure 5 Impact on surpluses of subsidy

Activities
Markets – how they work

Activity 1 is a common past question requiring only a simple understanding of two key definitions.

Normative statements are opinions/evaluative judgements, which cannot be verified by relating to real world information.

Positive statements are factual, although not necessarily true, and can be verified or falsified by testing.

Activity 1

Identify which of the following are **positive statements** and which are **normative statements**:

(a) 'Despite the rise in demand, the firm was unable to increase supply above 1000 units a day.'
(b) 'The government should intervene to stop the excessive levels of demand.'
(c) 'Indirect taxes are an unfair way to reduce consumption levels.'
(d) 'Indirect taxes on food will have a regressive effect, because they will take a larger proportion of disposable income away from poorer income groups.'

Activity 2

Using demand and supply analysis, illustrate the effect that each of the following changes could be expected to have on oil prices.

(a) Strikes by Venezuelan oil workers demanding larger pay increases.
(b) A recession in the US economy.
(c) A reduction in the daily quotas that OPEC allows its members.
(d) An increase in the price of natural gas, a good in joint supply to oil production in the North Sea.
(e) Unexpected cold spells along the east coast of the USA.
(f) An increase in the productivity of oil platforms in the Indian Ocean.

Activity 3

Draw demand and supply curves for a Nike branded T-shirt (Table 1).

Table 1

Price	Quantity demanded	Quantity supplied
£30	5,000	25,000
£25	10,000	20,000
£20	15,000	15,000
£15	20,000	10,000
£10	25,000	5,000

Pitfalls to avoid

Remember to get the elasticity formulae the correct way up or the answer will give you an inelastic co-efficient instead of elastic and vice versa. The percentage change in quantity demanded/supplied is always on the top of the sum.

(a) Where is the market equilibrium?
(b) How much total revenue will the producer make at this point?
(c) If the producer tried to charge £5 more for each T-shirt what would be:
  ■ the effect on the market?
  ■ the price elasticity of demand and the price elasticity of supply between the equilibrium and this new price?
  ■ the effect of the price increase on the total revenue of the firm?

Activity 4

The demand for Birds Eye frozen peas is assumed to be 40 million bags a year (worth £64 million in 1999, 40 per cent of the total UK market). Suppose that the income elasticity of demand for Birds Eye frozen peas is –0.5 and that the cross elasticity of demand for Birds Eye frozen peas with respect to the price of fresh peas is +2.

(a) What would be the impact of a fall in income of 5 per cent on sales? What would this tell you about the nature of the product?

(b) A bumper crop of fresh peas reduces their price by 30 per cent. What would be the effect on demand for Birds Eye frozen peas? What does the cross elasticity figure tell you about the relationship between the goods?

Activity 5

(a) What factors make the supply of fresh-cut flowers inelastic in the short run? Show the effect of Valentine's Day on the price of a bouquet.

(b) Why might flower supply become more elastic over a longer period?

(c) What would occur if a large number of producers entered the market?

Activity 6

What is the opportunity cost of an increase in capital goods from C to D (Figure 1) in the short run?

(a) FB
(b) OD
(c) OB
(d) BA
(e) ED

What is likely to be the long run impact of such a reallocation of our resources away from consumer goods and into investment into capital goods on our economy's production possibility frontier?

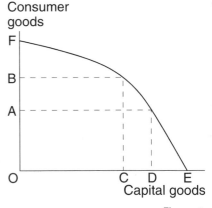

Figure 1

Activity 7

Assess different policies that a producer might try to make demand more price inelastic so giving the firm a greater price-raising ability in a market.

Answers
Markets – how they work

Activity 1

(a) Positive.
(b) Normative. The keyword 'should' indicates an evaluative judgement.
(c) Normative. The keyword 'unfair' indicates an opinion
(d) Positive. An economist could gather all the necessary information to verify or falsify the statement.

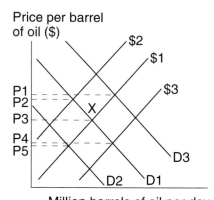

Price per barrel of oil ($)

Million barrels of oil per day

Figure 1

Definition

"

OPEC is the Oil Producing and Exporting Countries cartel. It aims to stabilise oil prices by the imposition of quotas onto the production of oil by its member nations and by the preservation of oil stocks to be released in times of deficient supply to the market.

Activity 2

Looking at Figure 1 and assuming that we start each time at the equilibrium D1, S1 at X:

(a) Venezuela is a major oil producer and therefore a disruption to supply will occur. Supply would shift to the left to S2 and the price would rise to P2.
(b) A recession will reduce the output of the US so that it requires less energy. The demand for oil will fall to D2 and the price will fall to P5.
(c) A reduction in quotas for **OPEC** members will decrease oil exports to other non-OPEC nations decreasing the supply to S2. The price would rise to P2.
(d) An increase in gas prices will make drilling for North Sea Oil more profitable. Thus supply will increase to S3 and price would fall to P4.
(e) Unexpected cold spells in the USA may mean that their demand for oil increases to generate more electricity. Therefore the demand would increase to D3 and the price would rise to P1.
(f) Increased productivity would mean that each oil platform generated oil at a cheaper unit cost of production. This would increase the supply to S3, reducing the price to P4.

Activity 3

Look at Figure 2:

(a) Demand = Supply at a price of £20 and quantity of 15,000.
(b) £20 x 15,000 = £300,000
(c) The market would produce a surplus of 10,000 at a price of £25.

$$PED = \frac{-50\% \text{ change in quantity demanded}}{+25\% \text{ change in price}} = -2$$

$$PES = \frac{+33.3\% \text{ change in quantity supplied}}{+25\% \text{ change in price}} = +1.3$$

The revenue would be the new price X quantity demanded at this price:

£25 x 10,000 = £250,000. Therefore it has fallen by £50,000.

Activity 4

(a) Income Elasticity of Demand =

$$-0.5 = \frac{? \text{ \% change in quantity demanded}}{-5\% \text{ change in income}}$$

Therefore the quantity demanded will increase by 2.5 per cent. They would sell 1 million extra bags of frozen peas. The good is *inferior* because the *YED* is negative.

(b) Cross Elasticity of Demand =

$$+2 = \frac{? \text{ \%change in quantity demanded}}{-30\% \text{ change in fresh peas price}}$$

Therefore the demand for frozen peas would fall by 60 per cent from 40 million to 16 million bags. The positive elastic *XED* figure indicates that the goods are close substitutes.

Activity 5

(a) The goods are perishable and cannot be stored for long. Their production time is long. It is not immediately easy to transfer resources into the production of flowers. Growers are likely to operate close to the capacity of their land and yield per acre.
Valentine's day will cause a dramatic increase in price since the demand increases but the supply is so inelastic.
(b) Over time more producers might move into the market. Given more time more crops can be grown. In the very long run, technology and plant yields may change.
(c) The supply would shift to the right reducing the price of fresh flowers.

Activity 6

Answer: (d) BA

The PPF will shift outwards in the long term as the investments into capital goods bring an increase in our potential production of both goods.

Activity 7

Advertising to increase brand loyalty. Other marketing schemes such as free gifts, add-on extras, credit schemes to differentiate his product will have the same effect as may quality improvements.

Reducing the amount of competitors in the market through mergers or predatory pricing schemes may also make demand more inelastic.

Definition

The opportunity cost is the highest valued alternative foregone when undertaking a particular decision. Here the increase in capital good output reduces the amount of resources available to produce consumer goods and output would fall by BA.

Exam hints

Activity 7 asks for some evaluation with the keyword 'assess' so something should be said about the cost of these activities or the fact that they take time to work. Mergers may be prevented by the competition authorities. Other firms may block your strategy with their own advertising.

Exam guidance and practice

Unit 1: Markets – how they work

Unit 1 is one-hour long, consisting of eight supported-choice questions and one data-response from a choice of two. It is worth 30 per cent of the overall AS grade. The marks are divided equally between the two sections, so it is sensible to try and spend half an hour on each. The timing is tight so you will have to be careful if you are to finish the exam. Note that the last question(s) on the data response tend to be worth more marks and it is vital that you get onto them if you are to perform to your potential. You may wish to attempt the data response first to make sure of this.

The supported choice section

Each question is worth 5 marks – 1 mark for the answer and up to 4 marks for quality of explanation. You should look to spend no more than 3 minutes on each question. This will give you a few minutes leeway at the end of the supported-choice section to read through the data responses properly. It is often a good idea to annotate the diagram, or to include your own diagram as part of your answer. Make sure that you label the axes fully. You should always try and include a full definition of any economic terms that are used in the question. Many of the questions will centre on the demand and supply diagram so make sure that you are confident using it.

The data-response section

Firstly, do not make the mistake that invariably some candidates make each year: only answer *ONE* of the two data responses! It is a good idea to read the questions first. This way you are already looking for answers in the passage when you read it for the first time. Do not be put off answering a data response because you may not know the answer to an opening question. These are normally to do with defining a term and are worth only a few marks. Look at the later questions where most of the marks lie. It is vital that you recognise the keywords in these questions. Twenty per cent of the Unit 1 marks are for evaluation and the last parts of the data response are the only section of the paper where this can occur. Although you can answer the questions in any order, there is normally a logical reason behind the question structure. This can sometimes help you answer the question. Note that if there is a chart or diagram in the data response, it is very likely that it can be incorporated into at least one of the answers. Allocate your time appropriately to the number of marks for each of the questions.

Pitfalls to avoid

One of the most common errors is to confuse an increase and decrease in supply. Note that when the supply shifts to the left, although it may appear to be moving up in the diagram, the level of quantity supplied is falling at every price level. This is a decrease in supply.

Boost your grade

Evaluation keywords include:
- assess
- to what extent
- evaluate.

You must:
- **assess** the relative importance of the point you are making
- **weigh up** the short and long run effects;
- **develop** a counter-argument.

Considering the elasticity is often useful to determine the magnitude of the effect.

Sample supported-choice questions

1   The owners of a local club estimate that the price elasticity of demand for entrance to their 1980s theme-night is –2.0. They expect 200 people

to come if they set the price at £10. Reducing the price to £9 can be expected to change their revenue by:

A −£2160   D +£160

B −£60   E +£2160.

C +£60

Answer: D

The price elasticity of demand measures the responsiveness of quantity demanded to changes in the price of the entrance to the club. It is measured by the formula

$$\frac{\%change\ in\ quantity\ demanded}{\%change\ in\ the\ price.}$$

The total revenue of the club is the price per ticket multiplied by the number of tickets sold. Initially £10 × 200 = £2000. Using the formula we can see that the 10 per cent reduction in the price will attract another 20 per cent customers to the club.

This means that: 200 + 20% = 240 people will come

240 × £9 = £2160: Therefore the total revenue will increase by £160.

2 The following data (Table 1) shows the relationship between the price of X and the quantity demanded of two other products Y and Z.

Table 1

Price of X (£)	Quantity demanded of good Y	Quantity demanded of good Z
20	100	200
30	80	240

Which of the following is most likely to apply?

A Y and Z are both substitutes for good X.

B Y and Z are both complements for good X.

C Y is a complement for X, Z is a substitute for X.

D Y is a substitute for X, Z is a complement for X.

E Y and Z are unrelated to good X.

Answer: C

The cross elasticity of demand measures the relationship between the price of one good and the demand for a different good. Here the cross elasticity between X and Y is NEGATIVE. Increasing the price of X reduces demand for Y. This indicates a complementary relationship. The cross elasticity between X and Z is POSITIVE, indicating that the goods are substitutes.

Exam hints

Credit could also have been gained here by stating that the demand was relatively price elastic, as the coefficient was greater than 1. This means that the reduction in price will lead to a larger proportionate increase in quantity demanded, so revenue could be expected to rise.

PART 2

MARKETS – WHY THEY FAIL

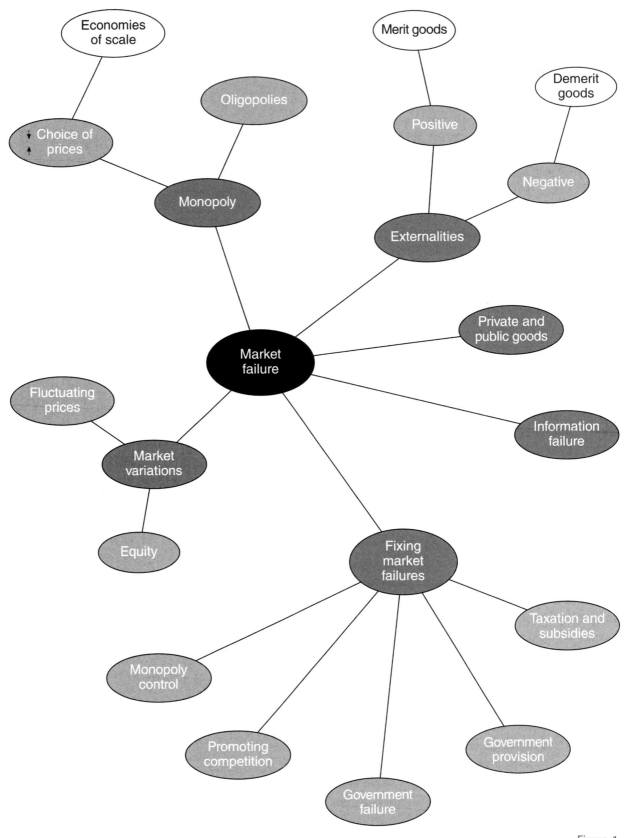

Figure 1

Top tips

- Make sure your file of stories about contemporary economic events that you began for the first unit includes up-to-date examples of externalities. Big environmental issues are usually well covered in all newspapers but try digging a little deeper by reading more academic articles. There is lots of stuff on the Internet about monopoly control.

Introductions are useful. When you read them for the first time, you may not understand everything. Don't worry. Work through the units and then read through the introduction a second time. If it still doesn't make sense, you should go and speak to your teacher or lecturer.

Market failure

2.2

In Section 1.2 (pages 18–19) you were introduced to a simple input-output model of how markets work and how they could achieve desirable outcomes. Some indications were given of the possible limitations of economic systems that relied solely on the market mechanism to solve the so-called economic problem of market failure. *Markets – why they fail* provides an introduction to what economists call market failure. It builds and extends the analysis you developed when tackling Part 1 *Markets – how they work.*

Recap on the advantages of the price mechanism

One of the most famous advocates of the **price mechanism** was Adam Smith (see Section 1.14). In his book *Wealth of Nations*, published in 1776, Smith argued that if all members of society pursued what they perceived to be their selfish interest:

> *The uniform, constant and uninterrupted effort of every man to better his condition, the principle from which public and national, as well as private opulence is originally derived, is frequently powerful enough to maintain the natural progress of things toward improvement, in spite both of the extravagance of government, and of the greatest errors of administration.*

In other words, society would improve if its individual members were left to their own devices. They would be driven, as if by instinct, to make profits from their activities. Those who were most successful would make the greatest profit. Those who were less successful would fail. Smith argued that an **'invisible [or hidden] hand'** linked producers to consumers and society as a whole. That invisible hand would help ensure that what was actually produced was what people wanted. In short, **allocative efficiency** would be achieved. Competition should also ensure that goods and services are produced at the lowest possible unit cost – **productive efficiency**. In this way the price mechanism is meant to ensure the optimum allocation of resources.

Factors preventing the success of the price mechanism

A number of factors might prevent these desirable outcomes. They can be considered under the following headings.
- **Monopolies**
- Merit and demerit goods.
- **Externalities.**
- Public goods.

Monopolies

Adam Smith identified the dangers of **monopoly**. He argued that:

> A monopoly granted either to an individual or to a trading company
> has the same effect as a secret in trade or manufactures. The
> monopolists, by keeping the market constantly under-stocked, by never
> fully supplying the effectual demand, sell their commodities much
> above the natural price, and raise their emoluments [income] whether
> they consist in wages or profit, greatly above their natural rate.

In other words, a monopolist would produce less more expensively than would
be the case if there were a number of producers competing against each other.

Merit and demerit goods

All societies make judgements as to what products and services are desirable
or undesirable. If markets were left to themselves these 'social valuations'
might be ignored. Thus, it could be argued that sales of illegal drugs would
increase if their supply were left to the market. Conversely, as there is little
profit in providing health care to the poor, their needs might be ignored.
Goods and services such as these which a society may judge to be 'good' or
'bad' are classified as **merit** and **demerit goods**.

Externalities

All economic transactions are likely to have third-party effects, which can be
both positive and negative. The benefits and problems associated with
producing and consuming particular goods and services are not necessarily
confined to the producer and consumer. Not only might improvements to
parking facilities, for example, benefit motorists and nearby store owners, but
also, if congestion is reduced, other transport users and people living in the
area could benefit. Conversely, a producer who can cut costs by dumping
waste products may inflict costs on innocent third parties. The market-based
price mechanism focuses on the immediate effects on producers and
consumers and is likely to ignore external effects. These **externalities** may be
very significant.

Public goods

The existence of externalities is linked to the concept of **public goods**.
Sometimes it is very hard to judge who benefits from the production of a
particular good or service. It can be argued that we all benefit from the
National Fire Service because of the protection it can provide in time of fire,
flood or other emergency. It is conceivable – although highly unlikely – that
some kind of cover might be provided by a freely operating market. Hence,
it is logical that this provision, along with the police and armed forces is
funded out of general taxation, provided by the government and is free at
the point of use. Services such as these are described as public goods.

Thinking like an economist

Students new to economics
often get public and merit goods
muddled up. Remember, merit goods
are linked to the valuation or
otherwise a society places on
particular outputs, whereas public
goods are those that are unlikely to be
provided by freely operating markets.

Hot potato

Would we all be better off if we
relied on market forces to
supply education?

Government intervention

2.3

No economies rely entirely on markets to allocate resources. Some, like the United States of America, are more competitive than others, but even there the government supports a vast arms industry and provides a range of benefits to farmers. The ex-communist countries like Czechoslovakia and Albania were dominated by state control, as is the case today in North Korea. Almost every country, therefore, relies on a mixture of state intervention and operation of the price mechanism. Typically, states take responsibility for armed forces, police and education. Many support agriculture and provide state-run insurance for the old and sick. Governments also intervene into markets. This intervention includes:

- the operation of **buffer stocks**
- subsidising farmers
- enforcing minimum wage levels.

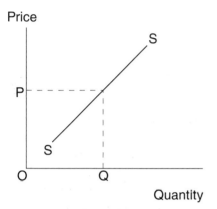

Figure 1 Using buffer stocks

Buffer stocks

Buffer stocks have been used for thousands of years in an attempt to iron out fluctuations in demand and supply. They can also be used to promote stability in markets in which there might be extensive fluctuations. If for some reason there is an increase in supply, a government could step in and purchase the commodity in question. If it can be stored, it can be held back from the market and released when there are shortages. In Figure 1, if the government wanted to keep prices around P, it would buy from producers if supply rose above Q, and sell from stocks if supply fell below Q.

Farm subsidies

These operate in a similar way to buffer stocks. Ever since the Second World War, governments in Europe have tried to ensure that long-term food supplies are ensured by promising farmers a particular level of income.

It was argued that agricultural production was a special case because of the impact on output of variations in the weather. Indeed, these variations could be magnified if farmers based production plans for one year on harvests and prices of the previous year. If there were a poor harvest, supply would fall, forcing prices up. If farmers believed that this price would apply the following year, they might be encouraged to increase production. If they then had a good harvest, output the next year would shoot up, resulting in falling prices. This is known as the cobweb process, and could actually intensify price instability.

Governments have tried to reduce uncertainty by guaranteeing minimum price levels for particular products. Therefore, if the minimum price was set at £120 per tonne for wheat, this would be the minimum return farmers receive. If the market equilibrium were to fall beneath this figure, governments could buy surplus wheat, forcing up the price. What governments do with these surpluses is a problem. If this happened repeatedly, governments would be left with large surpluses.

Minimum wages

Many countries intervene in labour markets to try to prevent workers from being exploited by working for low wages. Simple economic theory suggests that any attempt to introduce a minimum wage level above the equilibrium would increase unemployment. This is shown in Figure 2, where the equilibrium wage rate is given as W. If a government introduced a minimum wage of W1, this model suggests that the demand for workers would fall to E. Supply, however, would rise to E1, giving excess supply (or unemployment) of E to E1

The Labour government in Britain introduced national minimum wages in 1998. Currently, workers over the age of 18 should earn at least £3.60 an hour and workers over 22 at least £4.20 an hour. There has been little evidence that this has actually caused a rise in unemployment, which might show that this simple form of economic theory is wrong or may indicate that other factors, such as demand for labour, might have changed.

Summary

Governments may decide that market-determined outcomes are not in the best interests of the country or particular groups of people. There is a very high level of intervention around the world in agricultural markets. This might be to encourage price stability or protect farmers' incomes. Governments also intervene in an effort to prevent the exploitation of workers in industries where low pay rates are found.

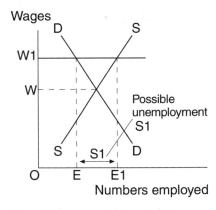

Figure 2 Government intervention

Thinking like an economist

The minimum wage example is a good illustration of how important it is for economists to back up their theoretical work with appropriate evidence. The observation that the re-introduction of a minimum wage in this country has not resulted in increased unemployment needs to be closely checked, especially in those industries in which rates of pay were poor.

> ### Puzzler
>
> How has the European Union managed to produce wine lakes, butter mountains and loads of frozen beef?

Economies of scale
2.4

One of the themes of your course is to help you judge whether or not current economic developments in the world are desirable. A key feature of contemporary developments is the tendency for firms to get bigger and bigger. One way of trying to judge whether big is better is by understanding both the benefits and disadvantages that can arise as firms get bigger.

As companies grow in size, there are factors that may reduce costs of production. It is cheaper, for example, for a large company like Tesco to sell milk than it is for your local milkman. Due to its increased size, Tesco will order more and so can negotiate bigger discounts. The cost reductions associated with a firm getting bigger are called **economies of scale**, and there are two types:
- internal
- external returns to scale.

Internal economies of scale

These relate to reductions in cost associated with the growth of an individual firm and can occur as a result of the following factors.

Technical factors

As firms grow, they may be able to afford and sell larger outputs, which make it 'economic' to use more efficient production techniques. For example, a wide-bodied plane such as the Airbus 300 series has lower running costs per passenger mile compared to a smaller plane such as the Boeing 707, because larger planes are more fuel-efficient. Similarly, as manufacturing firms grow and produce larger saleable outputs, they are likely to be able to afford more expensive but more efficient computer-driven automated production methods.

Organisational factors

The growth of firms and production of larger outputs enables the application of the division of labour and principles of specialisation. Those who work for small firms may have to undertake a range of jobs and will find it hard to develop cost-saving skills and expertise in particular fields. As companies grow, they can afford to employ specialists in finance and marketing and the like, and this can result in savings and falling long run average costs.

Growth and higher revenues can allow firms to invest more heavily in research and development. This is especially important in those industries in which the rate of change is rapid, such as electronics and pharmaceuticals. These sectors of the global economy tend to be dominated by giant firms such as Sony and GlaxoSmithKline. Their growth leads to greater research efforts, which lead to the development of new products and the establishment of new sources of competitive advantage.

Market power

Firms that grow can exercise more power in the various marketplaces in which they operate. Expanding output can allow companies to negotiate larger discounts from suppliers. In the UK, the major supermarkets are said to be able to force food suppliers to accept ever lower prices while maintaining ever higher standards.

External returns

These relate to changes in long-run costs that are associated with the expansion of a particular industry rather than an individual company. Long-run costs might fall if an industry expands in a particular area so that suppliers are attracted. This might lead to a reduction in the transport costs of components, for example. Alternatively, the grouping of related businesses in urban areas such as London generates additional costs of congestion and pollution.

Diseconomies of scale

Before you run away with the idea that big is better, there are factors that may make bigger firms less efficient and higher-cost producers. As firms grow, they become more complex, more difficult to manage and more impersonal to work for. Size is also associated with more red tape and bureaucracy, and communications can become slower and less effective.

There are advantages to not growing large. Small businesses may be more responsive to their customers. They can be more approachable and flexible, and their workers may be more motivated. Growth can also lead to rising long run costs or **diseconomies of scale**.

Large powerful companies can be the targets of unsatisfied customers. Shell, Nike and Exxon have all been targeted as they use their size to exploit both workers and consumers.

Evidence of diseconomies comes from those large companies like Marconi, which are on the verge of bankruptcy and by the trend of demerger, where large companies are often broken up, in the words of the financial press, 'to concentrate on core activities'.

Research task

Pick a large company such as Nike, Starbucks, Esso or IKEA and search the Internet for evidence of worker or customer dissatisfaction.

Summary

There is no automatic formula that can be applied to firms as they grow in size. In some industries, such as motorcar manufacture, potential economies of scale that benefit firms able to employ large-scale global production are enormous. In others, especially where more traditional methods of production are used, diseconomies of scale may be more significant.

Hot potato

Airbus industries is developing a 500–600 seat airliner. Is this good or bad news?

Monopoly power

I n the purest sense a monopoly exists when one organisation is the sole producer or provider of a good or service. A number of factors may give some firms more market power than others. In particular, there may be barriers to the entry and exit of firms from an industry. These include:

- ownership and control of raw materials
- patents
- economies of scale
- anti-competitive behaviour.

Ownership and control

If businesses are going to move freely in and out of industries in response to market pressures then they need access to the resources or factors required for production. If the ownership and control of raw materials is confined to a few companies, they can exert considerable control over that industry. The De Beers Group, for example, owns a significant number of diamond mines, and this has given it the means by which it can regulate the supply of diamonds and limit the impact of competitive behaviour. Similarly, oil reserves tend to be owned or controlled by a relatively small group of companies. This gives Exxon, Shell and the like great control of a series of oil-based industries.

Patents

Governments issue patents to help businesses enjoy the benefits of investing in and developing new products. Patents simply mean that it is against the law for other firms to produce the same products without permission from the inventor. In most countries inventors of new products or processes can apply for patent status, which can last for anything up to 25 years. It is said that Xerox took out hundreds of patents covering different working parts of its photocopiers to ensure that its monopoly lasted as long as possible.

Economies of scale

The concept of economies of scale was introduced in section 2.4. Put very simply, it means that larger firms can often produce goods more cheaply. This can give larger companies a considerable competitive advantage compared to smaller producers. This particularly applies when large investments in expensive machinery and systems are required. Thus, it is very hard for small music companies to compete with large companies such as Sony and EMI.

Anti-competitive behaviour

Most firms try to avoid competition. They indulge in different behaviours designed to limit it to prevent new firms from entering their industry. This can range from legal activities associated with building up strong brand images (See Figure1) to illegal price fixing and even strong-arm tactics.

Figure 1 The SONY brand image

Effects of monopoly power

Firms with monopoly power can charge higher prices, absorb higher costs and restrict customer choice.

Higher prices

If a company has monopoly power, it will have much greater freedom to set its own prices. This is probably something we take for granted. Prices are likely to be higher from a petrol station that has no local competitors. We pay for more branded goods than we do for non-branded goods. On the other hand, if there is lots of competition, individual companies will be strongly influenced by the prices charged by other businesses. Economists describe companies that have monopolistic power as **price makers**. If they know that the demand for their product is relatively inelastic, they can boost revenue by putting up prices.

Another aspect of market power is that a monopolist can also charge different customers different prices for the same product. So, a Mazda 323 is nearly £5000 more expensive in the UK than in the rest of Europe. This particular form of monopoly power is called **price discrimination**. Companies have used this technique to boost profits by charging higher prices to those with more **inelastic** demands and lower prices to those whose demand is relatively more **elastic**.

Higher costs

A monopolist will have less incentive to keep costs low. If a company is a price maker it can pass on additional costs to its customers, because higher prices absorb any extra costs associated with higher production. A firm with more competition, on the other hand, might be afraid that competitors will offer **substitute** products more cheaply.

Restricted choice

Monopolies can exploit the dependence of their customers on their products by restricting choice. Henry Ford was famous for saying that customers could buy a Model T Ford in any colour as long as it was black. More modern forms of this kind of behaviour include limiting the number of retailers allowed to sell particular products.

Thinking like an economist

When you analyse a market, ask yourself where you would place it on the following continuum:

Pure monopoly	Pure competition

Most markets will fall somewhere in the middle of these two extremes.

Web link

Visit: www.heinemann.co.uk/hotlinks and enter express code 0829P to find out about consumer and competition policy.

Quickie ✓

Conduct a survey of the cost of televisions in local stores. What evidence does this reveal of competition in this particular market?

Puzzler

Who provides the greatest choice on television: BBC or ITV?

Negative externalities

2.6

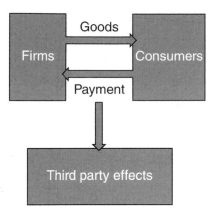

Figure 1 Third-party effects

Externalities are another concept used to analyse possible market failure. They are defined by economists as third-party effects of any transaction between a consumer and a firm. Externalities can either be positive or negative. It can be argued that if markets are left to themselves, too many goods and services will be produced that have harmful third-party effects, and too few goods and services will be produced that have beneficial third-party effects.

The potential existence of externalities is illustrated in Figure 1 in which consumers and firms transact with each other, the firms supplying goods or services for which they are paid. This transaction may have unintended third party effects which can be both harmful and beneficial.

Analysing negative externalities

A whole range of industrial and commercial activities can give rise to **negative externalities**.

Pollution of various kinds is one example. Some businesses may pay little regard to the effects of their activities on others. Clear and pure water might be used to cool, clean and wash, only to be returned to rivers and watercourses as pollution. Forests are exploited for their timber, giving rise to erosion, floods, infertility and even global warming. Anti-social behaviour by consumers of alcohol and tobacco can affect the well-being and health of 'innocent' third parties. These negative externalities are not just effects that are socially undesirable, they also represent additional costs for other members of society.

Negative externalities and market failure

The significance of negative externalities must be taken into account by economists and also when debating the strengths and weaknesses of the market system because their existence places additional costs on members of society. There are links, for example, between smoking tobacco and a range of serious diseases. Treatment of patients with these diseases means that the National Health Service (NHS) and private health insurance companies are faced with additional expenditure.

If markets operate freely and effectively, the price that a customer pays for a product or service should represent the actual costs involved in the production of that product or service. If production generates additional costs for other members of society, the market system can be said to have failed. This can be shown graphically. In Figure 2, **P** represents the costs of production faced by the producer of a good. These are known as **private costs**. **P1** includes negative externalities and, therefore, represents the total costs that the production of this product creates for society as a whole. This is known as the **marginal social cost** and represents the full cost to society of producing the product or service.

If there were no government or other intervention, equilibrium would be reached with price at **P** and sales of **Q**. However, if it were possible to calculate the external costs, these were added to the private costs and if consumers were required to pay the full social cost of production, a different equilibrium would prevail, giving a higher price of **P1** and reduced sales of **Q1**. In other words, a freely operating market would lead to lower prices and higher outputs of goods that have harmful environmental and/or social consequences.

Summary

Negative externalities exist when the marginal social cost of production exceeds the private costs of production. If no account is taken of their existence, the price mechanism would result in the underpricing of such goods or services. This would lead to higher levels of production than would be the case if the private costs reflected the full cost to society. Failure to take account of negative externalities would also mean that some members of society are faced with paying costs they have not incurred, such as passive smokers for example.

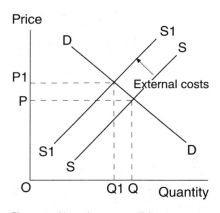

Figure 2 Negative externalities

Quickie ✓

Work in groups to brainstorm those economic activities that generate negative externalities.
(a) Choose three that your group consider the most harmful to third parties.
(b) Discuss as a class, and note if a consensus is reached or whether differences persist.

Puzzler *(and a hard one!)*

What link might there be between negative externalities and external diseconomies of scale?

Research task

Undertake an investigation of a market in which you consider there are significant negative externalities. How would you go about identifying and putting a price to the social costs you identify?

Web link

Learn more about externalities by visiting: www.helnemann.co.uk/hotlinks and entering express code 0829P.

Positive externalities

Unintended external effects do not automatically lead to greater costs for society as a whole. Some economic transactions generate beneficial third-party effects. Economists call these **positive externalities**. As you will see, it can be argued that the price mechanism is likely to under-produce goods and services that produce positive externalities.

Definition

Positive externalities occur when social benefits exceed private benefits.

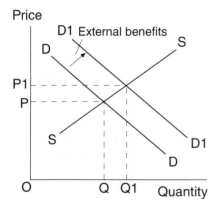

Figure 1 Positive externalities

Making connections

Why is fluoride added to toothpaste?

Analysing positive externalities

Positive externalities are slightly more difficult to identify than their negative counterparts. They are often associated with government or charitable interventions into the market. In the mid-nineteenth century, for example, local government in many British cities invested in the provision of clean, piped water. This had an obvious direct benefit to those who were given access to safe water supplies but it also contributed to better standards of health, less illness and disease, and greater productivity. In this way employers and society in general benefited. Similarly, improvements to education and training may benefit society as a whole as well as those individuals who are directly concerned with the improvements.

More modern examples would include the benefits to urban regeneration that follow if a significant national retailer decides to open a new branch in a particular area. Major stores like Boots or Sainsbury attract customers not just for themselves but also for other nearby retailers. Such increases in consumer spending will have other beneficial knock-on effects.

Graphical representations

The existence of positive externalities can also be illustrated graphically. In Figure 1, **DD** represents the demand from individuals, i.e. the private benefits gained from purchasing a particular good or service. **SS** represents the costs of providing that good or service.

The market equilibrium would lead to a price of **P** and sales of **Q**. If, however, it were possible to quantify the positive externalities associated with the provision of this good or service, these could be represented by **D1D1** showing the full **marginal social benefits** that would benefit society as a whole. If these additional benefits were taken into account, the equilibrium gives a new price of **P1** and sales of **Q1**. In other words, more would be produced. Thus, freely operating markets would ignore the benefits of positive externalities and less of such goods would be produced.

The growth of particular industries in specific areas can create external economies of scale, which will themselves contribute to positive externalities. For example, the growth of financial services in areas such as Bristol attracts more supporting businesses, such as those involved in software production. The concentration of a range of related businesses in a given area is likely to benefit all those involved.

Summary

Positive externalities exist when the marginal social benefits of production exceed the private benefits. If no account is taken of their existence, the price mechanism would result in the over-pricing of such goods or services, leading to lower levels of production than would be the case if the private benefits reflected the full benefits to society. Failure to take account of positive externalities would also mean that some members of society are gaining benefits for which they have not paid.

Definition

A marginal social benefit is the extra social benefit of increasing production by one unit.

Research task

Undertake an investigation of a market in which you consider there are significant positive externalities. How would you go about identifying and putting a price on the possible social benefits?

Quickie ✓

Work in groups to brainstorm those economic activities that generate positive externalities.

(a) Choose three which your group consider the most beneficial to third parties.

(b) Discuss as a class, and note if a consensus is reached or whether differences persist.

Public, merit and demerit goods

2.8

Definitions

A **public good** is one which can be consumed by more than one person, and from which everybody can benefit.

A **private good** can only be consumed once and is then not available for further consumption. Examples would be a packet of crisps or an area of land which is used to build a new housing development and is therefore no longer available for any other use.

Thinking like an economist

The unconstrained action of Adam Smith's hidden hand (the automatic allocation of resources by a free market) can lead to socially unacceptable outcomes. Consensus as to what is acceptable and what is unacceptable in terms of inequalities, the over-production of socially harmful goods and services, and the under-supply of socially valued outputs is very difficult to achieve.

Markets might be considered to fail if they result in the under- or over-production of certain types of goods. This can provide a reason for government intervention.

Under-production

The free market system might lead to under-production of:

- **public goods**
- **merit goods**.

Public goods

Some groups of goods and services that are likely to be under-provided by a free market system are public goods. These are products or services for which it is difficult to identify who benefits most, such as the police service.

In a free market, those who gain the greatest satisfaction from the consumption of a good or service are likely to be prepared to pay the most. In this way, resources are rationed out to those who believe they will benefit most. In some cases, it is impossible to predict who actually benefits from the production of particular goods and services. It is therefore hard to predict who needs the police and when, and it would be hard to work out a means by which consumers of police services would actually pay directly for the resources used. Another way of looking at the same issue is to argue that the social benefits of an effective police force are enormous and much larger than any private benefit.

Economists argue that public goods have two important features that differentiate them from other goods. The first is non-rivalry, which means that if one person consumes a good or service, others are not prevented from doing the same. So, one person enjoying Snowdonia will not stop someone else having a similar experience. Second, public goods are non-excludable, which is a related concept. This means that once a public good is provided to one person it is not possible to stop others from enjoying it, even if they don't pay for it. The market might be seen to fail here, as it won't produce the desired amount of public goods because they aren't being paid for.

Merit goods

The market system may also lead to the under-production of merit goods. These might be something society considers desirable, or might apply if production or provision were to create large positive externalities (see section 2.7) Prior to 1947, health services in the UK were provided by a free market. Those people needing a doctor had to pay and the poor often suffered ill-health because of this financial barrier. The Labour government elected in 1945 was committed to the notion of a free health service. Economists call this government provision of something that is socially desirable a merit goods. Merit goods include the provision of library services, job centres, state education, and health and recreational services.

Over-production

Consideration has already been given to circumstances in which companies will over-produce if private costs are far less than social costs, creating negative externalities. But, left to its own devices, a free market could also lead to the production of goods and services that a society might judge to be socially harmful. Measures are taken by governments to correct the market failure by reducing the consumption of commodities such as alcohol and tobacco. The provision of other goods and services such as cannabis, prostitution and offensive weapons is banned. Goods that are judged to be harmful to society are called **demerit goods**.

Government intervention

The existence of public, merit and demerit goods is a reason for government or others to intervene in the price mechanism to correct the market failure. Prior to the nineteenth century, public goods were provided by public donation. Lighthouses, for example, were first built by public subscription. The horrific consequences of shipwrecks made it possible in the eighteenth century for organisations such as Trinity House to raise sufficient funds to build lighthouses like the famous Bishops Rock. Schools were also set up on the basis of the generosity of the public and different Christian groups.

Towards the end of the nineteenth century, however, the government took an increasing role in the provision of education, road building and other public works. It used taxation to fund such investments.

Government provision of public and merit goods increased during the two world wars and in the 1930s, and continued to increase in the second half of the twentieth century. In more recent years, there has been vigorous political debate as to the effectiveness of such intervention. Conservative governments in the 1980s tried to reduce the role of the state, and the current government favours partnerships between the public and private sectors in the provision of health and some aspects of educational provision.

Other sources of market failure

2.9

Freely operating markets might not produce socially desirable or acceptable outcomes for other reasons. These include:

- **factor immobility**
- imperfect knowledge
- inequalities in the distribution of income.

Factor immobility

If markets are to work freely to allocate resources efficiently to those whose demand is greater then they should respond to the push and pull of the price mechanism. If the demand for a particular good increases, its price should rise – increasing potential profits for producers. Those producers will then increase their demand for factors of production and will offer higher wages for labour, higher rents for land, higher rates of interest for investment funds and greater profits to entrepreneurs. The increase in factor prices should act as a signal for the owners of factors to sell to the highest bidder. Factors of production should also move to those uses for which the demand is greatest. But do they?

This analysis assumes that factors move to the use wherever the return is highest. It is assumed that the profit motive outweighs other considerations. However, there is considerable evidence that humans do not behave solely in response to greater profitability. In practice it is often hard for workers to switch jobs or their work locations. Land and capital can be tied to particular uses. Managers and risk-takers are not only motivated by salary increases. For these reasons factors may be slow to move between alternative uses and are therefore less mobile or immobile. This means that freely operating markets rarely result in resources being used to produce those goods and services that are most in demand at a given moment.

Imperfect knowledge

If free markets are going to lead to optimum allocation of resources, all consumers and producers need to be well informed about the markets in which they are involved. It may be unrealistic to assume perfect knowledge and in reality knowledge and information may be very unevenly distributed. This concept is called **asymmetric information**, and economists have identified different examples of this possible imbalance.

One of the clearest examples can be drawn from the work of the American economist, George Akerlof, who analysed the relationship between the buyer and seller of used cars. He argued that the potential buyer would have very little understanding of the real quality of second-hand cars, whereas the seller would be far better informed. The potential transaction between the buyer and the seller would, Akerlof argued, be based on asymmetric information.

This principle can be applied to many different contexts involving the superior knowledge of sellers at the expense of the ignorance of customers and has been further developed in terms of the '**principal–agent problem**'. We do not always take economic decisions independently and often rely on the expertise of others. The person taking the decision is called the principal and the adviser is the agent. Thus, sorting out a pension plan is difficult and it is logical to seek help from a financial adviser. The adviser or agent may not necessarily be acting in the best interest of the principal. Financial advisers may give misleading advice because they have been paid incentives by particular companies to sell particular pension products. In this case, there is asymmetric information between principal and agent.

The effect of this is that a free market economy may allocate resources according to the preferences of those with most knowledge, rather than on an equal basis. For this reason markets might be said to fail.

Income inequalities

The significance of this potential source of market failure was introduced in section 1.16. Consumers need income to enter and take part in market transactions. In virtually every economy, however, income is unevenly distributed. Freely operating markets will not allocate resources to those who cannot afford to pay the market price. This may create conditions that are socially unacceptable. Some would argue that there are direct links between poverty and crime. It follows that if freely operating markets fail to deal with poverty, society as a whole will be faced with enormous external or additional costs and governments may need to intervene.

> ### Quickie
>
>
> What can be done to deal with the problem of asymmetric information?

> ### Puzzler
>
> Does it pay to deal with the causes of crime rather than its consequences?

Key concept

The principal–agent problem arises because in an increasingly complex world we rely on others to help us make economic decisions. Resources may then be allocated more heavily in favour of those with more knowledge.

Hot potato

Ask an older person about pensions and see what happens.

Remedies for market failure – monopoly regulation

There is a range of measures that governments may consider in trying to deal with market failure. These include:

- **monopoly** regulation
- the promotion of competition
- taxation and subsides
- tradable permits.

This section deals with monopoly regulation. The other measures are considered in the sections that follow.

The UK and most other world governments pursue two strategies in order to reduce the possible distortions to the economy caused by monopoly power. These are:

- limiting non-competitive behaviour by various constraints and controls
- encouraging competitive behaviour by trying to create competitive conditions in markets (see Section 2.11).

Limiting the power of monopolists

All western countries have policies that are intended to protect customers from the exploitation of monopoly power. In the UK these are the responsibility of the Secretary of State for Trade and Industry. There is considerable legislation designed to protect the interests of consumers and possibly limit the power of monopolists. In law, a monopoly exists if 25 per cent or more of sales in a given market are in the hands of one firm. There is a legal framework to ensure mergers that would result in gaining such a market share are investigated. These and other laws to protect customers are policed by the Competition Commission which was created by the government on 1 April 1999 in an attempt to strengthen consumer protection. This government body took over from the Monopolies and Mergers Commission.

The role of the Competition Commission

The Competition Commission's role is to investigate and report on matters referred to it relating to mergers, monopolies, anti-competitive practices, the regulation of utilities (public services such as gas and electricity) and the performance of public sector bodies. The Competition Commission cannot initiate its own inquiries. Most referrals have been made by the Director General of Fair Trading (DGFT), the Secretary of State for Trade and Industry, and the regulators of utilities. In almost all cases, the Competition Commission is asked to decide whether or not the matter referred was against the public interest.

The Competition Commission is a semi-legal body that considers evidence before making judgements as to:

- whether or not a particular firm or group of firms has acted in such a way as to violate any of the laws or regulations relating to that firm
- whether a firm or group of firms has acted in a non-competitive way and their actions are against the public interest.

The notion of the public interest is a legal recognition that although firms may be judged to be non-competitive there may be compensating benefits. The classic argument used by monopolists in defence of their activities is that, although competition is reduced, they are able to exploit economies of scale that lead to the supply of cheaper products than would otherwise be the case.

The Competition Commission reports directly to the Secretary of State for Trade and Industry and it is up to the government to decide on what action needs to be taken. The Commission also has powers to investigate mergers which would have the effect of creating monopoly power.

The problem of monopoly is such that there is extensive legislation designed to limit this form of market failure. For example, between 1973 and 1991 there were at least four different acts dealing with mergers alone.

Summary

Since the end of the Second World War, the UK government has enacted legislation designed to limit the abuse of monopoly power, especially in respect of protecting consumers from over-pricing and a restricted choice of products. It has been argued that the existence of monopoly power tilts the balance of the economy away from meeting the interests of consumers to meeting those of large powerful companies. The existence of monopolies, therefore, may also make an economy less efficient, both in terms of costs of production and of customers being able to buy the goods and services they demand, as there is no competition for prices.

Although the government has extensive powers to investigate the large firms, monopolistic behaviour is common in the UK economy. This may reflect the inadequacy of controls or the sheer impossibility of policing the activities of large firms.

Exam hint

You don't need to know the details of all the legislation, but you do need to understand that the government tries to establish what is in the public interest, and doing this involves balancing the advantages and disadvantages of monopoly – just the sort of question examiners like to ask.

Quickie

Why is there so much legislation about monopoly?

Remedies for market failure – promoting competition

A nother strategy followed by the UK and other governments to reduce the possible market failure caused by monopolies is to encourage greater competition. Many different strategies have been followed that try to encourage the growth of new firms and the easier entry and exit of existing firms into particular industries. These include:

- **privatisation**
- regulation
- creating internal markets
- encouraging enterprise.

Privatisation

In the early 1980s, the Conservative government led by Margaret Thatcher tried to increase competition by transferring the ownership of businesses such as BP from public to private ownership. In the mid-1980s, Sealink, Jaguar, British Telecom and British Gas were also sold. At the end of the decade and in the early 1990s, more complicated sell-offs such as the water, electricity and rail industries (see Figure 1) were undertaken. The intention of these changes was to promote greater allocative and productive efficiency. The success or otherwise of privatisation policies should be judged on the extent to which prices have been cut, output has been raised and choice has been increased.

The government believed that state ownership reduced the incentive for managers to be as efficient as possible, and the transfer to private ownership was meant to increase the importance that was attached to profitability. In addition to fitting in with the overall policy of encouraging more competition, privatisation created additional government revenue, which has been estimated to exceed £60 billion.

Regulation

One of the problems of privatising industries, especially those that were said to be natural monopolies, is that a publicly owned monopoly might simply be replaced with one owned privately. This was recognised by the Conservative governments in the 1980s, which tried to safeguard the public interest by creating a series of regulators. These are independent bodies such as OFCOM (Office of Communications), OFWAT (Office of Water Services) and OFGEM (Office of Gas and Electricity Markets). They have powers to regulate the actual behaviour of these industries by keeping a check on prices, insisting on customer service targets and levels of investment.

Internal markets

In the 1980s, the Conservatives realised that the total privatisation of the public sector would be both politically unacceptable and very difficult to implement. They choose instead a variety of strategies designed to introduce or mimic market forces within industries and organisations.

The creation of internal markets involves the creation of individual cost centres and greater independence in financial decision-making. In the NHS, budget-holding doctors were given the freedom to purchase medical care from those hospitals providing the most attractive service. Hospitals were expected to compete for business from GPs (doctors in local practices). This represented a radical change in established procedures that could have had devastating political effects had the government been prepared to allow failing hospitals to go bust and close. The incoming Labour government decided to limit the amount of competition in the health service, abandoning these policies in 1997 to allow more money and focus to be directed to patient care.

Related developments include forcing local councils and other government agencies to put the provision of services out to offer. In other words, competition between the public and private sector is created.

Encouraging enterprise

UK governments have placed considerable emphasis on encouraging more people to start up their own businesses to avoid monopolistic markets. They provide grants and advice to prospective small businesses and have tried to end practices that meant the entry of new firms into markets was limited. Thus, companies such as Specsavers can now provide competition to traditional opticians.

Summary

Public policy associated with trying to prevent the abuses of monopolistic power has involved a mixture of 'carrot and stick' approaches. Section 2.10 was devoted to legal controls on the ownership and structure of large companies. It implied that legal controls had not been strictly or consistently applied in the UK. More recent developments have focused more on privatisation, the encouragement of greater enterprise and the growth of small businesses to ward off market failure.

Figure 1 Virgin trains, an example of the effects of government-introduced privatisation upon the UK market

Hot potato

Has rail privatisation worked?

Government intervention – negative externalities and demerit goods

The possible existence of market failure provides governments with a reason to intervene in the free working of markets. In reality there are very few markets in which governments do not intervene.

Negative externalities

If governments wish to try to correct a negative externality such as pollution, or limit the consumption of a demerit good like tobacco, they can use:

- the price mechanism – taxation
- direct controls
- persuasion
- tradable permits.

There are positive and negative aspects to each of these approaches. One of the difficult tasks for governments (and economists) is anticipating the possible effects, intended and unintended, of particular actions.

Price mechanism – taxation

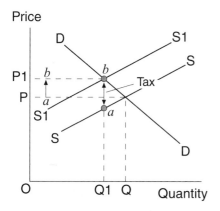

Figure 1 Taxing away negative externalities

This approach can be illustrated diagrammatically as shown in Figure 1.

If a government is able to calculate accurately the external costs attributed to a polluting company, it could introduce a tax equal to the vertical distance **ab**. This would force consumers of this product to pay a price that represented the full costs to society of its production. Output would be reduced to **Q1** and the government would actually use the price mechanism to cure market failure.

One advantage of this approach is that if it worked, it would strengthen market-based solutions. If the right price were chosen, it would be possible to ensure that customers actually paid for the true value of the resources used in the supply of the good or service. However, applying this principle to problems such as traffic congestion can create controversy and opposition from car users (see Figure 2).

Direct controls

Governments can choose to pass laws and use the existing legislative framework in an attempt to control and constrain the behaviour of firms and industries that generate negative externalities. In the UK, emissions of potentially dangerous chemicals are controlled by various regulations. Advertising by the tobacco industry is also limited, and car safety is promoted by annual car tests.

Figure 2 London's central congestion charges

The difficulty with rules or controls is that they can be broken and that a regulatory framework is required to ensure this does not happen. Direct controls are often applied to demerit goods. Do they work to stop young people consuming alcohol?

Persuasion

Some consider that changing customer and producer *behaviour* to ensure greater account is taken of externalities is so complex and difficult that it is more effective to change the *attitudes* of those who demand and supply products that create negative externalities (see Figure 3). The UK government, for example, part funds the Health Education Council, whose role includes encouraging people to eat healthier diets. If these approaches are successful, their effects will be fed through the market system. It is possible to argue that the increasing demand for organic produce is a result of greater awareness of the importance of a healthy diet.

Tradable permits

Another market-based means of limiting some negative externalities involves the government giving or selling permits to polluters to emit only a certain amount of waste. These permits can then be bought and sold. A company successful in cutting its pollution could sell its permit to one that was less successful. The company producing the lower emissions would gain by selling its permit and the heavier polluter would be forced to pay. By setting an overall limit regarding the amount of pollution allowed, governments could reduce this negative externality but it would be left to market forces to determine where emissions would be reduced.

There is a big debate among economists as to the effectiveness of such policies.

Figure 3 A victim of oil pollution and an example of a negative externality

Research task

Undertake an investigation of a market in which you consider there are significant negative externalities. How would you go about trying to estimate the monetary value on such externalities? Suggest possible government intervention strategies to take account of the externalities you have identified.

Quickie

In order of effectiveness, rank different strategies that could be used to reduce sulphur emission from power stations.

Hot potato

Has congestion charging in central London been a success?

2.13 Government regulation– positive externalities and merit goods

As outlined in section 2.7, the existence of positive externalities and merit goods might provide a justification for government intervention to make markets work more effectively. They can choose from a range of similar strategies to those used to deal with negative externalities. In this case the following strategies might be used:

- price mechanism – subsidies
- direct intervention – taxation
- persuasion
- vouchers.

Price mechanism – subsidies

Figure 1 illustrates a possible approach. A government might wish to work with the price mechanism to try to boost production of a product or service that provides positive externalities, which a free market might under-produce. It could estimate the value of the positive externality and pay a subsidy to producers equal to this amount to encourage production without raising prices. This is shown by the vertical distance *cd*. The outcome would be production rising from **Q** to **Q1** and price falling from **P** to **P1**.

If this approach were used to boost the sales of a merit good, its success or otherwise will partly depend on the elasticity of demand for the good or service. If the demand is relatively elastic, any reduction in its market price will result in a more than proportionate increase in demand. On the other hand, if demand is relatively inelastic a cut in price will have a smaller relative impact on sales, making such a policy less effective. These two possible outcomes are shown in Figures 2 and 3.

Direct intervention – taxation

If a government decides that the production of a particular good or service has significant positive externalities from which society may not fully benefit if markets were left to operate freely, it may intervene directly to provide that product or service. In many market-based economies, governments use taxation directly to provide merit goods such as education and health services. In these cases, sole reliance is not placed on freely operating markets.

In the UK, everyone is entitled to medical care. In terms of demand and supply, this means that the no direct payment is made and the government uses the NHS to try to provide whatever is demanded.

It is likely that UK society would not approve of a more market-based system that used prices to allocate health care or education because that would probably result in no health treatments or education for significant parts of the population who could not or would not pay for the service.

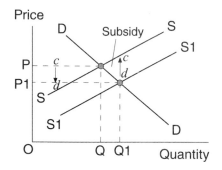
Figure 1 Using subsidies to account for positive externalities

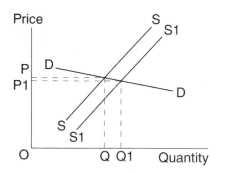
Figure 2 Elastic demand

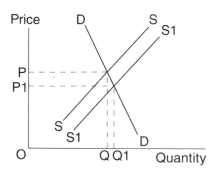
Figure 3 Inelastic demand

Persuasion

It could be argued that much of any government's work is concerned with persuasion in the form of advertising, political campaigning and the like. Changing attitudes to many aspects of our lives such as education, healthy living, sustainability, and preventive medicine, can all be seen as attempts to change free market outcomes. These approaches, however, work through the price mechanism by boosting demand for particular services or treatments.

Vouchers

Both Conservative and Labour governments in the UK have experimented with the use of vouchers, with the aim of producing greater consumption of merit goods or those with positive externalities. For example, the Labour government introduced Individual Learning Accounts in 1999, whereby adults were given a voucher up to the value of £150 to purchase additional education or training.

These vouchers are really an alternative form of money that can be given to those judged in need and used to purchase particular goods or services. They are, therefore, comparable to tradable permits as they are meant to use the price mechanism to produce socially desirable results. The Individual Learning Account scheme succeeded in attracting a considerable number of adults back into education but it was later discovered that it was being used fraudulently. Some providing training were able to claim that they had provided courses which had not actually taken place.

The Conservative party advocates the use of educational vouchers that parents could use to send their children to the school of their choice. The problem with schemes such as this is that using quasi-money can provide opportunities for fraud and misuse.

Summary

This section has been devoted to outlining strategies that governments could use to try to boost the consumption of those goods or services which are deemed desirable, either because they benefit many people or because they are considered to be socially desirable. Each strategy has problems, but it is unlikely that many people would consider that resources should be allocated to those who can most afford them. Such arguments are partly about what we might call social justice. As long as positive externalities exist, however, an economic case can be made for government intervention to ensure that the benefits of such production to society are maximised.

> **Quickie**
>
> In order of effectiveness, rank different strategies that could be used to encourage more adults to improve their literacy and numeracy skills.

Making connections

What are the global effects of government subsidies to cotton growers in the USA?

Research task

Undertake an investigation of a market in which you consider there are significant positive externalities. What would you have to do to estimate the monetary value on such externalities? Suggest possible government intervention strategies to take account of the externalities you have identified.

Hot potato

Is better health care for the elderly a benefit or cost to society?

Government failure

Price

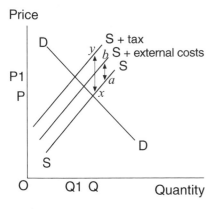

Figure 1 Over-taxing

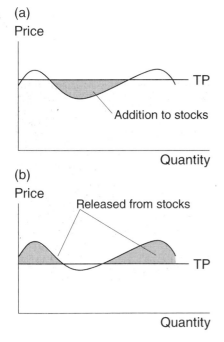

Figure 2 (a,b) The effects of wrong target prices

Government intervention to correct market failure does not always work. Indeed, it can even lead to a greater misallocation of resources. Policies might fail because of:

- inadequate information
- administrative failings
- unintended effects
- political conflicts.

Inadequate information

Many of the policy options outlined in Sections 2.12 and 2.13 rely on the government having excellent data and information on the markets in which they wish to intervene. If a government is using some form of tax to correct a negative externality, it has to be able to estimate accurately the external costs. If its estimates are too high then the market will be further distorted. This is shown in Figure 1, where the additional tax is set at xy rather than ab. This results in consumers paying more than the product is worth in terms of resources used.

Similarly, failure to set target prices at the right level will result in the failure of buffer stock policies, as can be seen in Figure 2 (a,b) where TP = target price. In the first of these diagrams, the price is set too high, resulting in ever bigger stocks; in the second, the price is set too low and buffer stocks would soon run out.

Administrative failings

Governments and civil servants make mistakes. The imposition of any control or regulation provides scope for evasion as people will try to avoid payment. Policing emission controls is very difficult and in many cases the penalties for non-compliance are not very strong deterrents.

Changing the behaviour of people involves affecting complex and deep-rooted attitudes. Public relations campaigns do not always work in the ways in which they were intended. Although some are far more successful than anticipated, many depend upon the coincidence of other events. From 1999–2003, the British government faced problems while trying to gather more evidence about the effectiveness and safety of GM foods. This is an example of a government attempt to change attitudes that many believe failed.

Unintended effects

The growth of unofficial markets is a good example of unintended effects, especially if the result of government policies is to create shortages of goods that are in demand. Unofficial markets arise when maximum prices are set so that shortages of products with negative benefits are created.

Some customers are prepared to pay more than the set price, which also creates a unofficial market for products such as ivory. In times of war, governments often seek to control market prices to ensure economic stability and make unofficial marketeering illegal. If governments introduce maximum prices during times of war, they usually outlaw unofficial markets. As unofficial markets are illegal, lawlessness is encouraged and this may have further repercussions. Much of modern gangsterism in the USA is said to have developed in the 1920s and 1930s when many states banned the consumption of alcohol. Demand was still high, leading to the creation of unofficial markets and, consequently, illegal activity.

The incentive for unofficial markets to develop is shown in Figure 3 in which the supply of a good is fixed at Q. Some customers are prepared to pay up to P1, which may indicate great profits from illegal activity.

Political conflicts

Politics can be seen as a means of reconciling conflicts. Politicians need the votes of voters who may have different objectives and therefore need to provide compromises. In 1999, the government announced that not all cigarette advertising was to be banned as quickly as originally intended. It has been argued that groups such as those promoting Formula 1 motor racing have been able to persuade the government to change its policies. In this case, there was a conflict between the Labour Party raising revenue and its desire to reduce smoking. In 1998, Bernie Ecclestone, the head of Formula 1, made a donation of £1 million to the Labour Party. This came at the same time as the government decision to exempt motor racing from an EU directive banning tobacco sponsorship in sports (Figure 4).

The jobs of politicians can be made harder as a result of the pressure that can be put on government by the media, various pressure groups and lobbyists. Sometimes politicians just cannot win.

Reconciling political differences is even harder in an international or global context. This is particularly significant in dealing with negative externalities. Pollution and pollutants do not recognise national boundaries. Countries need to agree common approaches. The failure of the US government to cut greenhouse gas emissions is considered by some to be one of the biggest threats facing the global economy.

Research task

What would be the implications on the agriculture industry of moving towards a much more market-based economy by ending government indirect taxes and the provision of subsidies?

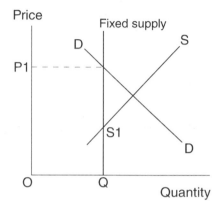

Figure 3 The potential for unofficial markets

Figure 4 Bernie Eccleston, head of Formula 1

Quickie

Was Adam Smith right about his concept of an ideal freely operating market?

2.15 Activities Markets – how they fail

Activity 1

Explain how each of the following types of potential market failure will affect output in a free market. Will there be under-production or over-production?

- The presence of public goods.
- Negative externalities.
- Demerit goods.
- Positive externalities.
- Monopoly power.

Activity 2

Fill in the grids by giving practical examples of market situations in which the following different types of externalities might occur.

Definition

Consumption externalities occur when a consumer cares about another agent's production or consumption. They can be positive externalities that give the third party consumer additional satisfaction or negative externalities that cause dissatisfaction to the third party consumer.

Definition

Production externalities occur when a producer cares about the activities of another, otherwise unrelated, agent's production or consumption. Positive production externalities would reduce this third party producer's costs. Negative production externalities will raise their costs.

	Negative effects on a third-party consumer.	Positive effects on a third-party consumer.
Externality caused by a producer.	e.g. The noise pollution from a local pub holding a karaoke-night keeps residents awake.	
Externality caused by another consumer.		

	Negative effects on a third-party producer.	Positive effects on a third-party producer.
Externality caused by another producer.		e.g. Cropspraying by a neighbouring farmer reduces the likelihood of pests attacking your crops and may directly benefit you by drifting in the wind onto your crops.
Externality caused by a consumer.		

Activity 3

Explain which of the following projects in Table 1 the government should select when considering the proposals to build a new bypass around a town.

Table 1

Project	Private benefits	Private costs	External benefits	External costs
A	1000	800	400	600
B	2000	1200	200	800
C	1500	1000	300	200
D	1800	1400	800	1200
E	1600	1400	800	600

Activity 4

The following data (Table 2) shows the marginal benefits, costs and marginal external costs of the production of a good that causes atmospheric pollution as a by-product of its production process. Assume that the firm seeks to equate the marginal social benefits with its marginal costs.

Table 2

Output	MSB Marginal social benefit	MC Marginal (private) costs	MEC Marginal external costs
0	0	0	0
1	20	8	8
2	18	10	8
3	16	12	8
4	14	14	8
5	12	16	8
6	10	18	8

Exam hints

Remember that the socially optimal level of output occurs when the MSC= MSB. Social costs are the sum of the individual producer's private costs and the environmental/external costs that the firm's production imposes on others. Similarly social benefits = private benefits + external benefits.

If the government were to try to 'internalise the externality' by the introduction of an indirect tax levied on the firm at the level of the marginal external cost, what would be the impact on the market output?

Answers
Markts –
how they fail

Definitions

Pure public goods are characterised by the conditions of non-excludability – the inability to prevent anyone from consuming them, and non-rivalry – one individual's consumption does not reduce the amount available to others. Therefore people will not voluntarily pay for public goods and governments must step in to provide them

Activity 1

- The presence of **public goods** is likely to result in their under-provision in a free market. Insufficient resources will be allocated to produce them, as free-riding will result in the inability of a private firm to get the revenue necessary to fund them.
- Negative externalities will result in over-production of the product in the absence of government intervention. Social costs will not be borne fully by the agent that produces the externalities.
- Demerit goods will also be over-consumed in a free market. Governments feel that individuals will not take the full damage that they incur from the consumption of these goods into account and that the goods must be regulated or taxed to restrict their consumption.
- Positive externalities will result in under-production, as the agent that causes the positive externality will not receive the full social benefit from their actions.
- Monopoly power will also tend to result in under-production, as monopolists are normally assumed to drive prices higher by restricting the supply of the product to the market. If a monopolist benefits from significant economies of scale, which reduce the firm's unit costs enough, it is possible that a monopolist could produce more than a competitive free market would.

Activity 2

Consumption externalities – examples

	Negative effects on a third-party consumer.	Positive effects on a third-party consumer.
Externality caused by a producer.	Noxious smells from a local sewerage treatment plant lower the quality of life and property values of the neighbourhood.	The construction of a new underground line providing easier commuter access into a city raises the value of properties around the new stations.
Externality caused by another consumer.	The eating of hot fast-food or use of a mobile phone in a crowded train or bus annoys other passengers.	Getting inoculated against a disease also prevents you becoming a carrier who can pass the disease onto others.

Production externalities – examples

	Negative effects on a third-party producer.	Positive effects on a third-party producer.
Externality caused by a another producer.	Acid rain from UK smokestack power generators imposes costs on timber firms in Norway.	The manure from a local stables might be given to farmers for compost for free.
Externality caused by a consumer.	The use of cars causing congestion raises the transport costs of firms trying to distribute their produce.	The use of the Internet, or subscription to a magazine by individuals might lower the costs of other firms trying to reach them with advertising.

Activity 3

Answer: Project C

This is an exercise in cost–benefit analysis, requiring the weighing up of the full social costs and benefits of different projects. Find the project with the highest net social benefit (social benefits – social costs).

Social benefit = private + external benefits, Social cost = private + external costs. The net social benefit is:

A   1400 - 1400 = 0
B   2200 - 2000 = 200
C   1800 - 1200 = 600
D   2600 - 2600 = 0
E   2400 - 2000 = 400

Activity 4

In a free market, the producer would only look at his marginal private costs and would therefore produce until the MSB = MPC. This would give an output of 4 units. Once he has to pay a tax equal to the MEC as well, he will now face a MSC = MC + MEC. This means that his MC will rise by eight at each level of output. MSB now equals MSC at an output of 2 units.

Exam hints

Remember that the allocatively efficient level of output occurs where the marginal social cost is equal to the marginal social benefit. If the MSB > MSC then the next unit of output would yield some more net social benefit. When the MSB = MSC, the net social benefit is maximised.

Markets – how they fail

Unit 2 is one hour long and consists of one extended data response passage from a choice of two. It is worth 30 per cent of the overall AS grade. It is therefore crucial that you spend the first 5–10 minutes properly reading through the two passages to make the correct choice. As with Unit 1, it is sensible to read the questions first so that you are looking for the answers during your first read through of the passages. Do not choose the passage simply because you think that you prefer the topic it is discussing. Your choice must be based on your ability to tackle the specific questions that have been set. The later questions are likely to be worth the largest proportion of the marks, therefore you should allocate your time accordingly to them. Again there will be some evaluation required in the last parts, so it is important that your answer is not simply explaining one side of the argument.

Sample data response: the Landfill Tax

The Landfill Tax was introduced in October 1996 and is levied on waste deposited in landfills. The objectives of the tax are to:

- encourage waste producers to minimise the volume of waste generated
- reduce the amount deposited in landfills
- encourage recycling.

A distinction was made between inactive waste, which, in 1996, was taxed at £2 per tonne, and other waste charged at the standard rate of £7 per tonne. In the March 1999 budget, the Chancellor announced that the standard rate would be raised from £7 to £10 a tonne and would be subject to a landfill tax escalator of £1 per tonne per year for at least another five years, reaching £15 per tonne in 2004. This is designed to increase the incentive to re-cycle or incinerate waste.

Landfill Accounts for around 90 per cent of controlled waste in the UK. Each year, 90–100 million tonnes of waste are sent to landfill. Landfill is regarded as the only option for some inert wastes and for wastes that are difficult to burn or recycle. Landfills can release chemicals into surface and underground water and soil, and generate methane which is a 'greenhouse gas'. The noise from increased traffic of heavy lorries also creates external costs as does the odour and visual inconvenience. There is also the risk of contamination of land and surrounding water. The risk of having a baby with a chromosomal abnormality such as Down's syndrome is increased by 40 per cent for women who live within 2 miles of toxic landfill sites, according to EU researchers.

Companies can claim back up to 20 per cent of landfill tax payments if they have made contributions to environmental projects that help to mitigate the

Exam hint

This provides the information for question 3. It is an attempt to 'make the polluter pay', to internalise the externality through a tax, so that the waste management firm is forced to pay the full social costs of its activities.

Exam hint

This part of the article contains the answer to question 1. Define negative externalities as the spill-over costs to local residents of the landfill disposal by the waste firms. Social costs exceed the private costs of the firms. Explain several of these external costs in your answer.

effects of their dumping of waste. However investigations into the regulation of these projects have exposed a significant amount of fraud and collusion between waste management companies and these environmental trusts. Millions of tonnes of waste are also being illegally dumped to avoid the tax. Alternatives to landfill, such as incineration, are often costly or impractical. Research from the EU and US experience suggests that the maximum economically efficient level of recycling is 40 per cent.

Adapted from HM Customs and Excise website.

www.hmce.gov.uk/forms/notices/lft1.htm

1. Define the term negative externalities using examples from the articles.
2. What is meant by the 'economically efficient level of recycling?'
3. Explain how the landfill tax was intended to reduce the incidence of these negative externalities.

Some hints

Note the information in the margin points to help with Questions 1 and 3. You should draw out the full MSC/MSB diagram for negative consumption externalities as part of the answer to question 2. This shows that the optimum level of recycling is not 100 per cent, but rather where the benefits from further recycling of waste are no longer sufficient to compensate for the extra social costs. The cost of further recycling would be greater than the value of damage that would be caused to the environment by not recycling. This diagram can also be used to tackle question 3 to show that the efficient level of landfill disposal can be reached as long as the level of the government taxation is set equal to the marginal external cost (the distance between the MSC and MPC). This would make the polluter pay the full social cost of landfill disposal rather than the firm's lower private costs.

Boost your grade

You will often have to draw and explain the marginal social benefit/costs diagram at some point in the exam, so make sure that you are familiar with how to illustrate both positive and negative externalities. Note the deadweight welfare loss triangle always 'points' towards the efficient equilibrium.

Part 2 Further reading

2.1

S. Munday, *Markets and Market Failure*, Heinemann, 2000, Chapter 4.

G. Hale, *Labour Markets*, Heinemann, 2001, Chapter 3.

C. Bamford, *Transport Economics*, 3rd edition, Heinemann, 2001, Chapter 6.

D. Burningham & J. Davies, *Environmental Economics*, 3rd edition, Heinemann, 2004, Chapter 2. Revised edition of D. Burningham & J. Davies, *Green Economics*, 2nd edition, Heinemann, 1999.

2.2

S. Munday, *Markets and Market Failure*, Heinemann, 2000, Chapter 6.

D. Burningham & J. Davies, *Environmental Economics*, 3rd edition, Heinemann, 2004, Chapter 7. Revised edition of D. Burningham & J. Davies, *Green Economics*, 2nd edition, Heinemann, 1999.

2.3

S. Munday, *Markets and Market Failure*, Heinemann, 2000, Chapter 4.

2.4

S. Munday, *Markets and Market Failure*, Heinemann, 2000, Chapter 4.

C. Bamford & S. Munday, *Markets*, Heinemann, 2002, Chapter 7.

C. Bamford, *Transport Economics*, 3rd edition, Heinemann, 2001, Chapter 4.

2.5

S. Munday, *Markets and Market Failure*, Heinemann, 2000, Chapters 4 and 9.

C. Bamford, *Transport Economics*, 3rd edition, Heinemann, 2001, Chapter 3.

D. Burningham & J. Davies, *Environmental Economics*, 3rd edition, Heinemann, 2004, Chapter 2. Revised edition of D. Burningham & J. Davies, *Green Economics*, 2nd edition, Heinemann, 1999.

2.6

S. Munday, *Markets and Market Failure*, Heinemann, 2000, Chapters 4 and 9.

C. Bamford, *Transport Economics*, 3rd edition, Heinemann, 2001, Chapter 3.

D. Burningham & J. Davies, *Environmental Economics*, 3rd edition, Heinemann, 2004, Chapter 2. Revised edition of D. Burningham & J. Davies, *Green Economics*, 2nd edition, Heinemann, 1999.

2.7

S. Munday, *Markets and Market Failure*, Heinemann, 2000, Chapters 4 and 8.

C. Bamford, *Transport Economics*, 3rd edition, Heinemann, 2001, Chapter 4.

2.8

S. Munday, *Markets and Market Failure*, Heinemann, 2000, Chapters 4 and 5.

D. Burningham & J. Davies, *Environmental Economics*, 3rd edition, Heinemann, 2004, Chapters 2, 3 and 4. Revised edition of D. Burningham & J. Davies, *Green Economics*, 2nd edition, Heinemann, 1999.

2.9

S. Munday, *Markets and Market Failure*, Heinemann, 2000, Chapter 6.
D. Burningham & J. Davies, *Environmental Economics*, 3rd edition,
Heinemann, 2004, Chapters 6, 7 and 9. Revised edition of D. Burningham &
J. Davies, *Green Economics*, 2nd edition, Heinemann, 1999.

2.10

S. Munday, *Markets and Market Failure*, Heinemann, 2000, Chapter 6.
C. Bamford, *Transport Economics*, 3rd edition, Heinemann, 2001, Chapter 5.

2.11

D. Burningham & J. Davies, *Environmental Economics*, 3rd edition,
Heinemann, 2004, Chapters 6, 7 and 9. Revised edition of D. Burningham &
J. Davies, *Green Economics*, 2nd edition, Heinemann, 1999.
S. Munday, *Markets and Market Failure*, Heinemann, 2000, Chapter 6.

2.12

S. Munday, *Markets and Market Failure*, Heinemann, 2000, Chapter 6.
D. Burningham & J. Davies, *Environmental Economics*, 3rd edition,
Heinemann, 2004, Chapters 6, 7 and 9. Revised edition of D. Burningham &
J. Davies, *Green Economics*, 2nd edition, Heinemann, 1999.

2.13

S. Munday, *Markets and Market Failure*, Heinemann, 2000, Chapter 7.
C. Bamford, *Transport Economics*, 3rd edition, Heinemann, 2001, Chapter 7.
D. Burningham & J. Davies, *Environmental Economics*, 3rd edition,
Heinemann, 2004, Chapter 9. Revised edition of D. Burningham & J. Davies,
Green Economics, 2nd edition, Heinemann, 1999.

PART 3
MANAGING THE ECONOMY

Managing the economy – an overview

Definition

Aggregate is used to mean total, i.e. the total demand of a country.

Figure 1 John Maynard Keynes (1883–1946)

John Maynard Keynes was born in 1883 in Cambridgeshire and is one of the best-known Economists. Keynes developed a critique of traditional laissez-faire economic theory and provided the framework for post-war economic recovery at Versailles in 1919. US President Franklin D. Roosevelt's 1930s New Deal was also a result of Keynesian theory.

Managing the economy is concerned with macroeconomics, which is the performance of the whole economy. How well the economy performs affects all our lives. It influences the quantity and quality of goods and services we can enjoy, our chances of gaining a job and the prices we pay for products.

In Part 3 you will first explore the key measures of economic performance, the key objectives of government policy and what is called **aggregate demand and aggregate supply** analysis. You will see some similarities with the demand and supply analysis you are familiar with from Part 1, including the widespread use of diagrams. However, it is important to realise that there are differences as you are now analysing total economic activity and not the market for just one product. For instance, on a demand and supply diagram the price of a product is measured on the vertical axis; however, on an aggregate supply and aggregate demand diagram the vertical axis is used for the price level. On the horizontal axis of the aggregate supply and aggregate demand diagram it is real GDP (Gross Domestic Product, or national output) that is measured, and a particular level of output is represented by Y.

You will also come across two different schools of economic thought: Keynesian and new classical. Keynesian economists are named after the famous twentieth-century economist, John Maynard Keynes (Figure 1). They think that there can be significant market failure and that in the absence of government intervention, the economy may experience significant macroeconomic problems. In contrast, new classical economists think that market failure is not significant and that the economy tends to move towards full employment in the long run. Due to their views on how economic forces work, Keynesians tend to favour government intervention, while new classical economists tend to urge a reduction in government intervention.

Sections 3.10 to 3.14 allow you to explore the main government policy objectives in more depth. You will consider the causes and consequences of unemployment, inflation, a current account deficit, economic growth and inequality in income distribution. Finally, the last sections focus on the key policies that can be used in the management of the economy, a sample examination paper and some useful examination guidance.

Tackling this unit

When you have completed this module you will be able to:
- explain how the performance of an economy is measured
- compare the performance of the UK economy with other economies

- explain the causes and consequences of economic growth, inflation, unemployment, balance of payments deficit and inequality of income
- apply aggregate demand and aggregate supply analysis to explore current economic behaviour and issues
- assess fiscal, monetary and supply-side policies.

Try to learn as you go along rather than leaving everything to the end. Read each section at least three times – once straight through, a second time to make sure that all the arguments and concepts are really understood, and a final time for reinforcement. The spider diagrams in Figures 1 (a, b, and c) that follow on pages 104–5 give an overview of the three main areas of Part 3. It would be useful to review these again at the end.

You might also begin reading the financial sections of newspapers and take advantage of magazines, periodicals and websites to help broaden your economic understanding. Additionally, it will be useful to look at the Edexcel website, which has good advice.

Web link

Go to the following website and enter express code **0829P** for more information about the question papers: www.heinemann.co.uk/hotlinks.

Revision tactics

A typical student will take around 12 weeks to reach the required standard when studying this unit. It will take that long to get used to applying aggregate demand and supply analysis, and to understand, analyse and evaluate measures of macroeconomic performance, policy objectives and policy measures. You will need a good grounding in the underpinning theory and concepts, as well as a good grasp of exam techniques, before you are fully ready to prepare for the unit test. The data-response questions will assume that you understand the whole of the unit. Take your time with exam preparation and work through the exam practice sections after you have been through Part 3.

Quickie

To get you started, think about the following points.
- What causes unemployment?
- Does inflation matter?
- What can the government do to improve the UK's international trade performance?
- Are living standards rising?

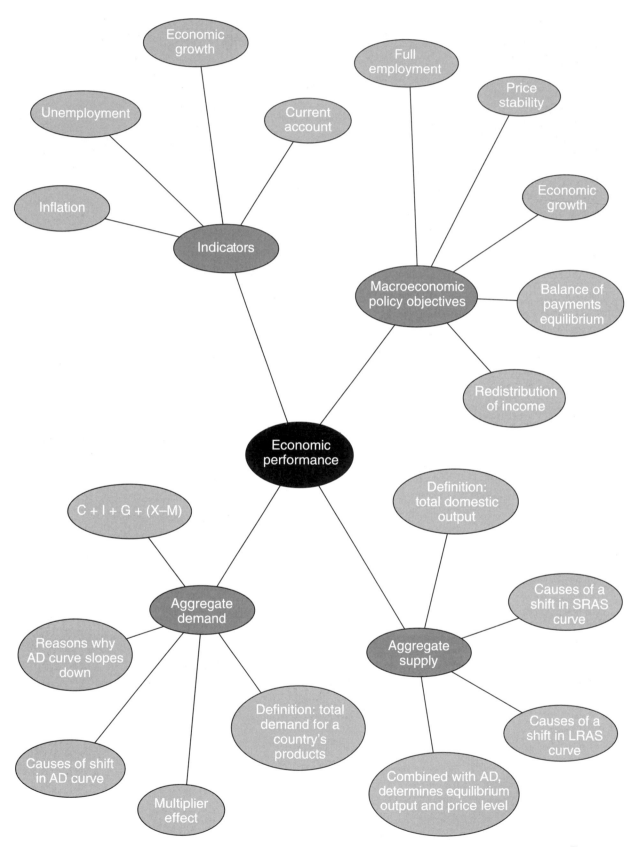

Figure 1a

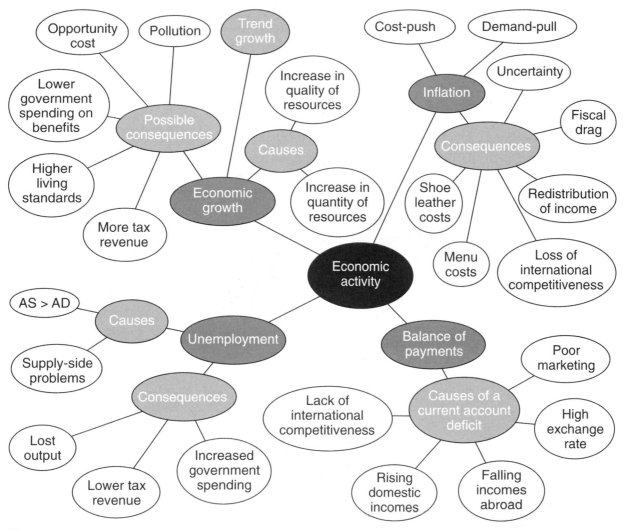

Figure 1b

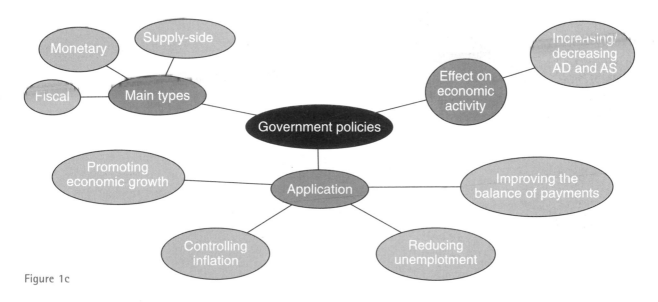

Figure 1c

Measures of the economic performance of countries

conomists compare the performance of the UK with other national economies by examining a number of key indicators – including economic growth, inflation, unemployment and the balance of payments. In this section you will see how these indicators of the health of the economy are measured.

Economic growth

Economic growth is measured as the change in real **Gross Domestic Product (GDP)**. Real GDP can be measured by totalling up the output, income or expenditure of the country.

When using the output measure, it is important to avoid counting the same output twice – for example, including the output of raw materials and then including it again in the value of finished products. In the income method, only incomes that have been earned in return for producing products are included, so pensions are not included. With the expenditure measure it is important to remember to include exports (as they are produced by domestic firms) and to exclude imports (as they are produced by other countries' firms).

Real and money (nominal) GDP

To assess economic growth it is important to use real GDP. A real figure (one measured in constant prices) is one that has been adjusted for inflation. The GDP of a country, measured in the prices operating in the year in question (money GDP), may rise from, say, £500,000 million in 2003 to £550,000 million in 2004. This would appear to suggest that output has risen by:

$$\frac{£50,000}{£500,000} \times 100 = 10\%$$

But if the price index in 2003 was 100 and 106 in 2004, real GDP was:

$$£550,000m \times \frac{100}{106} = £518,867.92m \ (= \text{rise in volume})$$

In real terms GDP has risen by 3.77%.

Economic growth rate

The economic growth rate is the percentage change in real GDP. Countries do not always experience steady economic growth. There can be booms, which are characterised by a high, unsustainable economic growth rate, low levels of unemployment and accelerating inflation. There can also be recessions. In a **recession** aggregate demand is usually falling, unemployment is high and output is declining. A common definition of a recession is a period of falling real GDP that lasts for at least six months.

Inflation

The **inflation** rate is the percentage change in the general price level and shows changes in the cost of living. It should be considered over time and in comparison with other countries' rates. This is relative inflation.

To measure the rate at which prices are changing, governments construct price indexes. In the UK the main price index is the **Retail Price Index (RPI)**. It is a weighted consumer price index. This means that changes in the prices of goods and services that people spend more on are given more importance (greater weighting) than those on which they only spend a small amount.

The government uses the data it collects in its compilation of the RPI to construct another index. This is the RPIX. It is the RPI minus mortgage interest payments.

Unemployment

There are two main measures of unemployment in the UK. One is the claimant count, which includes anyone who is receiving Jobseeker's Allowance. However, it misses some of those who are involuntarily unemployed as some unemployed people are not entitled to unemployment benefits, such as those aged under eighteen. The other measure is the Labour Force Survey (LFS) measure. This uses the International Labour Office (ILO) definition, which includes those without a job and who are actively seeking employment.

The balance of payments

The **balance of payments** is a record of a country's transactions with other countries over the period of a year. The section that receives the most media attention is the current account, which includes exports and imports.

Another main section is the financial account, which shows the movement of direct investment (e.g. the purchase of a factory), portfolio investment (e.g. the purchase of shares) and other investments (e.g. bank loans).

Web link

Visit the Office for National Statistics' website by going to www.heinemann.co.uk/hotlinks and entering express code 0829P.

Quickies

- What is the difference between real and nominal GDP?
- What is RPIX?
- What is meant by the unemployment rate?
- Which section of the balance of payments receives most attention?

Puzzler

Why do you think some economies perform better than others?

Interpretation of measures

C are has to be taken in interpreting the measures of economic performance. In this section you will examine some of the limitations of the key measures.

The Retail Price Index (RPI)

The RPI aims to give a representative picture of what is happening to prices in the UK. However, there are a number of reasons for believing that it may not give a totally accurate picture.

To assess whether prices are rising, the prices of the same products should be compared over time. However, products change, often improving in quality. So, for example, if the price of a vacuum cleaner rises, this may reflect a higher charge to cover improvements in the model rather than the same vacuum cleaner becoming more expensive.

Government officials also do not monitor prices in charity shops or car boot sales and not all Internet purchases. A limited range of Internet purchases were incorporated for the first time in February 2000, and gradually more are being added. As a result, the RPI may overstate the price rises that people face.

Another problem can arise when changes in the RPI are used to assess inflation because attempts to reduce inflation may in themselves raise it. One of the main categories in the RPI is housing, which includes mortgage interest rate repayments. When the Bank of England raises interest rates, it raises the cost of mortgage interest repayments and so, at least in the short run, raises the inflation rate. It is for this reason that the government uses the RPIX as its inflation target.

Unemployment measures

The **claimant count** includes some people who are working in the hidden economy (undeclared economic activity) and are illegally claiming Jobseeker's Allowance. It probably misses even more people who are genuinely unemployed. This is because some of those willing to work and who are actively seeking employment are not entitled to receive unemployment benefits.

The **Labour Force Survey (LFS)** measure is a more inclusive measure and, as it is used in many countries, it makes international comparisons easier. However, it takes time to conduct the LFS and process the information gathered. The survey is carried out every quarter (every three months) and the data is usually not produced until three months after the quarter to which they apply. The method is also subject to errors with the samples.

Definition

The claimant count is a measure of unemployment that includes those receiving Jobseeker's Allowance.

The Labour Force Survey (LFS) is a household survey that collects a range of information on the labour force. In deciding who is unemployed from the responses given, this measure uses the ILO definition.

Changes in real GDP and living standards

On the surface, an increase in real GDP may appear to suggest that living standards are increasing, but this may not be the case.

One problem of interpretation that economists can eliminate is that a rise in output may be exceeded by a rise in population. If there is, for example, 4 per cent more output and 7 per cent more people to share the output between, an average person will be worse off. So what economists often assess is real GDP per head. This is found by dividing real GDP by population.

However, there are other problems involved in comparing a country's real GDP over time and between countries. One is the existence of the hidden economy. The output of a country is likely to be higher than its official real GDP figure suggests. Some people selling goods and services may not include all the money they have earned on tax returns and those engaged in illegal activities will not be declaring any of the income from such activities.

As well as the size of the real GDP, its composition also has to be considered. If more is produced but the extra output consists of capital goods, people will not immediately feel better off, although they will in the long run. If the rise in real GDP has been accounted for by increasing the police service to match rising crime, people may actually feel worse off, as they would rather have less crime.

A rise in real GDP may not benefit all of the population if income is very unevenly distributed. Higher output may also result in people feeling the quality of their lives has not improved if they are working under worse conditions. The official figures do not take these factors into account. Nor do they include **positive** and **negative externalities**. If pollution rises, for example, real GDP does not fall, even though people will experience a lower quality of life. Indeed, if measures have to be taken to cope with the higher pollution, such as cleaning oil from beaches, real GDP will rise as more factors of production are used.

Balance of payments

Compiling the balance of payments involves collecting information on a vast number of activities that result in money entering and leaving a country. Mistakes can be made and some transactions may not be reported in time. For this reason, governments include a section in their balance of payments for errors and omissions.

Web link

For UK statistics go to www.heinemann.co.uk/hotlinks and enter express code 0829P.

Thinking like an economist

Discuss in what circumstances a fall in real GDP may be accompanied by a rise in living standards.

Quickies

- Identify two reasons why the RPI may overstate price rises.
- Explain one advantage of both the claimant count and the Labour Force Survey measures of unemployment.
- What is meant by real GDP per head?
- Identify two problems involved in compiling the balance of payments.

3.4 Macro-economic policy objectives

Government policy objectives and the emphasis placed on them can change as government administrations and economic theories change. However, the main objectives for the economy (macroeconomic objectives) pursued by most governments are:

- price stability
- full employment
- a steady rate of economic growth
- a satisfactory balance of payments.

Price stability

The UK government has given the Bank of England responsibility for achieving a 2.5 per cent target on the RPIX measure, with a 1 per cent margin either side. This is to enable low and stable inflation in order to ensure that prices are relatively stable.

A high and accelerating rate of inflation can be harmful to an economy. It may reduce the international price competitiveness of the country's products, may lower the real value of some people's incomes and savings, and is likely to create uncertainty, making planning difficult.

However, zero inflation, with the general price level remaining unchanged, has always been regarded as difficult to achieve and not particularly desirable. A low level of inflation, rather than zero inflation, may bring benefits – e.g. it may enable firms to reduce their costs by not raising wages in line with inflation rather than making some workers redundant.

Full employment

Unemployment involves a waste of resources, a loss of potential output and gives rise to a number of social problems – including poverty, crime and deviance. In contrast, high employment confers a number of important advantages, including the possibility of high output and high living standards. The highest possible employment may be referred to as **full employment**. This, however, does not mean zero unemployment, as there will always be some people who are between jobs.

A steady rate of economic growth

A steady rate of economic growth may provide advantages in an economy, including increasing material living standards. It also enables a government to reduce poverty without having to lower the living standards of the rich and middle income groups. This is because higher output will mean higher total income, some of which can be used to increase the employment opportunities of the poor – for example, by providing training and increased benefits.

As well as steady economic growth, governments are now increasingly aiming for **sustainable economic growth**.

Definitions

Full employment is a situation where those wanting to work can gain employment at the going wage rate – often taken as an unemployment rate of 3 per cent.

Sustainable economic growth is economic growth that does not endanger future generations' ability to expand productive capacity.

Satisfactory balance of payments position

In the long term, a government may seek to match revenue and expenditure on the current account of the balance of payments. However, in the short term, it may be content to see a deficit or a surplus. For example, a deficit may arise when an economy is expanding and buying more raw materials that will be converted into finished products – some of which will be exported. The deficit may also be offset by a surplus on another section of the balance of payments.

Other objectives

- **Income redistribution:** Governments seek to redistribute income from the rich to the poor. This is to reduce poverty and to ensure that everyone can participate in society. The extent to which a government tries to redistribute income is influenced by its view on the unfairness arising from the free market distribution of income and the extent of labour market failure.
- **Improving the environment:** Governments are also increasingly reflecting the concerns of their population and setting targets for looking after and improving the environment.

Influencing factors

One influence on a government's ability to achieve its macroeconomic objectives is the level of economic activity. An economic boom, for instance, is usually associated with a significant rise in real GDP and falling unemployment.

The level of economic activity in the UK's main trading partners also influences the UK government's ability to achieve its objectives. If the US, Japanese, German and other EU economies are performing well, they are likely to buy more products from the UK. This should help the UK's current account position, employment and economic growth rate.

Another influencing factor is the appropriateness of government policies. For instance, it would be inappropriate for a government to cut income tax when a country is experiencing high inflation. This is because the reduction in income tax will increase total demand in the economy and may raise the general price level even further.

Hot potato

Between 1998 and 2001 the price level in Japan fell. This caused major problems there. Consumers delayed their purchases, expecting prices to be lower in the future. Lower spending resulted in higher unemployment and falling output. The situation became so desperate that the Japanese government tried to generate inflation so that consumers would spend more, so preventing prices from falling further!

Quickies

- What is the government's inflation target?
- Why is there always some unemployment?
- Why may a government seek to redistribute income?
- Identify two factors that would make it easier for a government to achieve its objectives.

Aggregate demand (I)

In exploring what determines the level of economic activity in a country and economic problems and issues, economists use aggregate demand and aggregate supply analysis. In this section you will explore aggregate demand.

Aggregate demand

Aggregate demand is the total demand for a country's goods and services at a given price level. Demand comes from:

- people buying products such as clothing and food – consumption (C)
- firms buying capital goods, e.g. machines, delivery vehicles – investment (I)
- the government buying goods and services, e.g. educational materials, medicines – government spending (G)
- foreigners buying the country's goods and services (X) minus domestic demand for foreign goods and services (M) – net exports (X-M).

Aggregate demand (AD) is often expressed as:

$$AD = C + I + G + (X-M).$$

In this section you will look at consumption and investment.

Consumption

Consumption is the largest component of aggregate demand. The main influence on consumption is income. As income rises, consumption is likely to increase – although the proportion spent usually declines when people become richer. This is because they are able to save a higher proportion of their income. Other influences on consumption include the age structure of the country, inflation, the rate of interest and expectations about the future. For example, a fall in the rate of interest will encourage some people to spend more. This is because they will gain less from saving, it will be cheaper for them to borrow and they will have more money left to spend each month when they have made their mortgage repayment.

Investment

Investment is the component of aggregate demand that fluctuates the most. Gross investment is the total amount spent on capital goods. Again, the main influence is income. When income is increasing, demand for consumer goods and services is also likely to be rising. So firms will want to expand their capacity to meet this higher demand by purchasing capital goods.

Investment is also influenced by expectations. Demand may be high and rising but if firms expect that the increase in demand will slow down or reverse, they will not invest in capital goods and may not even replace all the capital goods that wear out.

Firms are likely to invest more when profits are high. They will have the finance and incentive to purchase extra capital goods in order to expand capacity. A fall in the rate of interest should stimulate investment. It will reduce the cost of borrowing funds to spend on capital goods and will reduce the opportunity cost of using retained profits for investment purposes. Firms will also be encouraged to buy capital goods if they fall in price and if advances in technology make them more productive than existing ones.

Quickies

- What is the difference between consumption and investment?
- Identify two influences on consumption.
- What effect would a rise in the rate of interest have on consumption and investment?

Puzzler

How do some people manage to spend more than their income?

Aggregate demand (2)

3.6

A ggregate demand (AD) comes from consumption, investment, government spending and net exports, and is expressed as:

$$AD = C + I + G + (X–M).$$

Here you will look at government spending and net exports.

Government spending

A government purchases a range of goods and services – including equipment and books for state schools, equipment for NHS hospitals and equipment for the armed services.

The amount a government spends depends on a number of factors. These include its views on the extent of market failure and the ability of state intervention to correct it; the electorate's demand for health, education, roads; and the level of activity in the economy.

Net exports

Demand for a country's exports, relative to its demand for its imports, is influenced by a range of factors. These include the price and quality competitiveness of its goods and services, incomes at home and abroad, marketing and the exchange rate.

The aggregate demand curve

The aggregate demand curve shows the total quantity demanded at different price levels (see Figure 1).

The aggregate demand curve (AD) slopes down from left to right, indicating that the lower the price level is, the higher aggregate demand will be. This is because a fall in the price level will do the following things.

Definition

Net exports are the value of exports minus the value of imports.

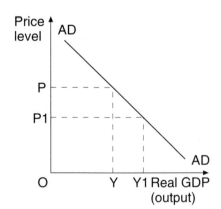

Figure 1 Extension in aggregate demand

- Make the country's goods and services more price competitive at home and abroad, so net exports will rise.
- Increase the amount that people's wealth can buy. This will encourage them to spend more and so raise consumption. (This is sometimes referred to as the wealth effect.)
- Cause interest rates to fall, and lower interest rates encourage a rise in consumption and investment.

Shifts in aggregate demand

If the aggregate demand curve shifts to the right, it means that the total demand for goods and services has increased for some reason other than a change in the price level. A shift to the left represents a decrease in aggregate demand, as shown in Figure 2.

You have already come across some of the reasons why the components of aggregate demand may change. For example, advances in technology will encourage firms to demand more capital goods. Other causes of changes in aggregate demand are changes in the size of the population and changes in the money supply.

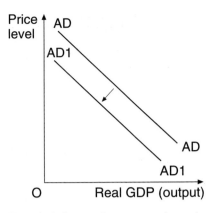

Figure 2 A decrease in aggregate demand

Quickie

Explain whether you would expect the following to shift the aggregate demand curve to the left or right.
(a) A rise in expected profits.
(b) A fall in income tax.
(c) A world recession.
(d) A rise in corporation tax (tax on firms' profits).

Exam hint

Be very careful with the labelling of AD diagrams. Remember, it is the price level on the vertical axis, real GDP on the horizontal axis and the curve shows aggregate demand. You will not get any marks for micro-labels. Also remember that while a change in the price level will cause a movement along the AD curve, a change in any other influence on AD (e.g. a change in the exchange rate) will cause in a shift in the AD curve.

Aggregate supply (1)

Aggregate supply is the total quantity of goods and services that the country's resources produce at a given price level. An aggregate supply curve shows the quantity of goods and services that would be produced at different price levels. Economists distinguish between short run aggregate supply and long run aggregate supply. This section will look at short run aggregate supply.

Short run aggregate supply

Short run **aggregate supply** is the total quantity that will be supplied at different price levels when the prices of factors of production are assumed not to be changing. Figure 1 shows a short run aggregate supply (SRAS) curve.

The curve shows the relationship between real output and the price level. It slopes up from left to right. There are two ways of looking at this.

One is to explain why the price level rises when output goes up. The reason is because while the wage rate, for example, is assumed not to be changing, marginal costs may rise with output. This is because to increase output, overtime rates may have to be paid and machinery may have to be worked at a faster rate, leading to more breakdowns.

The other is to explain why aggregate supply should rise when the price level goes up. If prices do increase while the prices of factors of production remain constant, production becomes more profitable.

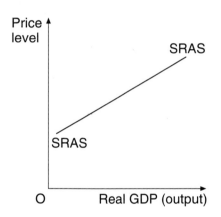

Figure 1 Short run aggregate supply curve

Shifts in short run aggregate supply

While a change in the price level will cause a movement along the AS curve, a change in any other influence on aggregate supply will cause a shift in the AS curve. A movement to the left of the SRAS curve shows a decrease in aggregate supply, whereas a shift to the right shows an increase. Figure 2 illustrates an increase in short run aggregate supply.

The main causes of changes in short run aggregate supply are:
- changes in import prices
- changes in the productivity of factors of production
- changes in taxation on firms.

These, of course, all change firms' costs of production.

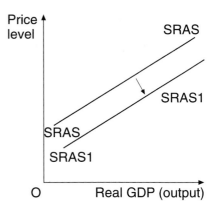

Figure 2 Increase in short run aggregate supply

Quickies

- What does an SRAS curve show?
- What effect would a rise in the price level have on SRAS?
- How would a fall in raw material costs affect SRAS?
- What effect would the discovery of new oil fields be likely to have on SRAS?

Puzzler

How could the government seek to increase SRAS?

Exam hint

As with AD diagrams, be very careful with the labelling of AS diagrams – price level on the vertical axis, and real GDP on the horizontal axis.

3.8 Aggregate supply (2)

As you saw in Section 3.7, aggregate supply is the total quantity of goods and services that the country's resources produce at a given price level. This section looks at long run aggregate supply.

Long run aggregate supply

Long run aggregate supply is the total quantity supplied at different price levels over a time period when the prices of the factors of production can change. For instance, the wage rate can move up or down.

Different views on the shape of the long run aggregate supply curve

Keynesian economists believe that the shape of the long run aggregate supply (LRAS) curve can be perfectly elastic at low levels of economic activity, less elastic at higher levels and perfectly inelastic when full employment is reached. This view is illustrated in Figure 1.

When the level of output is very low, and hence unemployment very high, between 0 and Y, any increase in output can be achieved by offering unemployed workers jobs at the going wage rate and paying the going price for materials and capital equipment. Between Y and Y1 shortages of workers, particularly skilled workers, and materials and equipment cause firms to compete for their services by offering to pay more for them. This raises costs and the price level. At Y1 all resources are employed and it is not possible to produce any more, however high the price level rises.

In contrast, new classical economists believe that in the long run the economy will operate at the full employment level and the LRAS curve will be vertical, as illustrated in Figure 2. Their thinking is that if, in the short run, aggregate demand falls, the workers who are made redundant will accept pay cuts and so price themselves back into employment in the longer run. So when the economy is operating at the long run equilibrium position, no one who is prepared to work at the going wage rate will be unemployed.

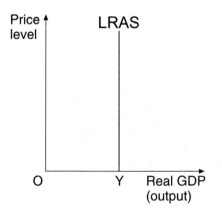

Figure 1 Keynesian long run aggregate supply curve

Figure 2 New classical long run aggregate supply curve

Making connections

Compare the LRAS curve with the production possibility curve (see Section 1.3). All the factors that would shift a production possibility curve to the right would also shift the LRAS curve to the right.

Shifts in long run aggregate supply

An increase in long run aggregate supply is illustrated by a shift to the right of the LRAS curve and a decrease by a shift to the left. Figure 3 (a,b) illustrates the Keynesian and the new classical views of an increase in LRAS.

A move to the right of the LRAS curve shows that the productive potential of the economy has increased. With its resources fully employed, an economy is capable of producing more goods and services. There are two main reasons why LRAS could increase.

One is an increase in the quantity of resources. For instance, an increase in married women's participation in the labour force will increase the supply of potential workers and net investment will increase the quantity of capital goods available.

Another is an increase in the quality of resources. So, for example, advances in technology and improvements in educational achievements will increase the quality of capital and labour and thereby raise their productivity.

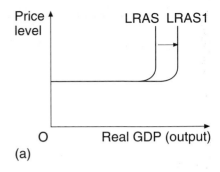
(a)

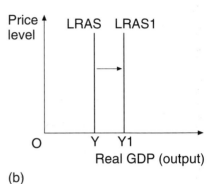
(b)

Figure 3(a,b) An increase in long run aggregate supply. (a) Keynesian view, (b) New classical view

Figure 4 Advanced technology in action

Quickies

- What does it indicate if the LRAS is vertical?
- What does a shift to the right of the LRAS curve indicate?

Puzzler

Raising the retirement age would be politically unpopular but the UK government is thinking of raising it to 70. By considering the effect on LRAS, identify a benefit to society of such a move.

The multiplier effect

3.9

The circular flow of income is an economic model that illustrates how the macroeconomy works. As you will see below, it can be used to analyse the causes and effects of changes in economic activity. It can also be used to explain how initial changes in aggregate demand result in greater final changes in aggregate demand.

The circular flow of income

In the simplified version of the **circular flow** of income shown in Figure 1, there are two sectors – households and firms. Between these two move (flow) income, spending, products and factor services. Households provide factor services such as labour and enterprise. In return, households receive incomes. They use these incomes to buy products produced by firms.

Injections and leakages

In practice, not all the income that is earned is spent and there are additional forms of spending that do not arise from the circular flow. Income that is not spent on domestic output leaks out of the circular flow. There are three **leakages** (which can also be called withdrawals). These are taxation, savings and spending on imports. Leakages reduce aggregate demand as there is less money to spend on goods and services. In contrast, **injections** increase aggregate demand. Again, there are three – investment, government spending and exports. These are additional forms of spending, arising outside the circular flow of income. When the value of injections equals the value of leakages, output will not be changing and there will be macroeconomic equilibrium.

The multiplier effect

When injections exceed leakages, aggregate demand will increase. This rise in aggregate demand will have a greater final effect on the economy. This is because when households, firms and the government spend money, that

Definitions

A **circular flow diagram** is a macroeconomic model of the movement of money, products and factor services around the economy.

Leakages are withdrawals from the circular flow.

Injections are additions to the circular flow.

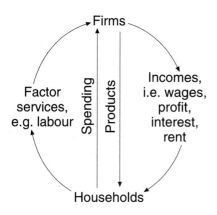

Figure 1 The circular flow of income

expenditure becomes the income of those who sell them the products. They in turn will spend some of the money they receive. So there is a knock-on effect, with aggregate demand rising by more than the initial amount. For example, if the government increases the value of pensions, the pensioners are likely to spend more on heating, housing and holidays. Those selling these products will receive more income. Some of this income will be spent and some will leak out of the circular flow. Spending will continue to rise until leakages match the initial injection. This is known as **the multiplier** effect and is measured in figures. A multiplier figure of 3, for instance, would mean that an injection of spending of £2 million would cause aggregate demand to rise by £6 million.

Of course, the **multiplier** effect also works in reverse. A rise in income tax, for instance, reduces disposable income and so reduces consumption. Lower spending causes firms to cut back on production, and reduces income and spending on wages. The lower income in turn reduces aggregate demand further.

The significance of the multiplier effect

The existence of a multiplier effect means that a government has to recognise that any change in government spending or taxation will have a knock-on effect on the economy. So that, for instance, if the government wants to raise real GDP by £10 billion and the multiplier has been estimated at 2, it would have to raise its spending by £5 billion.

Quickies

- What are the three possible injections into the circular flow?
- Why is saving a leakage from the circular flow?
- In what sense does spending create income?
- What would it mean if a country has a multiplier of 3?

Definition

The multiplier is the process by which any change in a component of aggregate demand results in a greater final change in real GDP

Thinking like an economist

Using an AD and AS diagram, explain what effect an increase in expenditure on imports would have on output, employment and the price level.

Hot potato

The size of the UK multiplier is thought to be around 1.93.

3.10 Equilibrium level of real output (1)

Macroeconomic equilibrium occurs where aggregate demand and aggregate supply are equal. When aggregate demand and aggregate supply are equal, there is no reason for national output (real GDP) and the price level to change.

Short run equilibrium

The short run equilibrium of output and the price level occurs where aggregate demand equals short run aggregate supply, as shown in Figure 1. At the price level of P, all the output produced by domestic firms is sold. There is no reason for producers to increase or reduce their output and there are no pressures pushing up or lowering the price level.

If, however, aggregate demand was higher than aggregate supply, there would be a shortage of goods and services (see Figure 2). Consumers would bid up the price level and the higher prices on offer would encourage firms to expand their output until equilibrium is restored.

Aggregate supply exceeding aggregate demand would also lead to pressures that would eventually move the economy back to equilibrium, as shown in Figure 3. This time, the existence of unsold goods and services would push the price level down. The lower price level would cause aggregate supply to contract and aggregate demand to expand until the two are equal.

Long run equilibrium

Economists agree that the long run equilibrium output and price level of an economy take place where aggregate demand equals the long run aggregate supply. However, they disagree about what this level of output may be.

Definitions

Macroeconomic equilibrium is a situation where aggregate demand equals aggregate supply and real GDP is not changing.

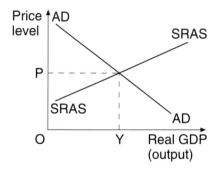

Figure 1 Short run equilibrium output

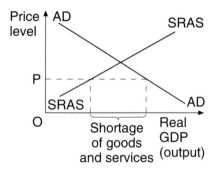

Figure 2 Aggregate demand exceeding aggregate supply

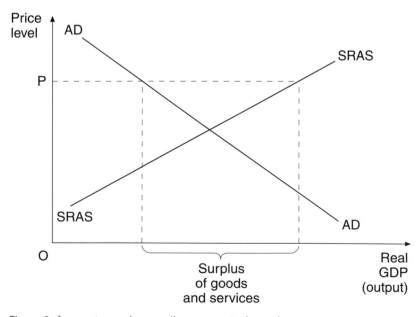

Figure 3 Aggregate supply exceeding aggregate demand

New classical economists argue that in the long run, the economy will operate with full employment of resources. As we saw in section 3.8, they believe that the long run aggregate supply curve is vertical. Figure 4 illustrates their view on long run equilibrium, with AD equalling LRAS.

Keynesians argue that aggregate demand may be equal to long run aggregate supply at any level of employment. They believe it is possible for an economy to be operating with spare capacity (with unused resources) if there is a lack of aggregate demand. Figure 5 shows long run equilibrium output occurring well below the full employment level. They also believe that the economy may be in equilibrium where it is experiencing shortages of resources and so where the price level is beginning to rise. They accept that it is possible for equilibrium output to be where full employment is achieved, but that this is only one of a whole range of possible output positions.

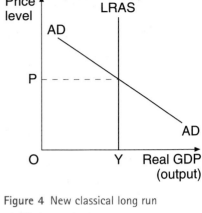

Figure 4 New classical long run equilibrium output

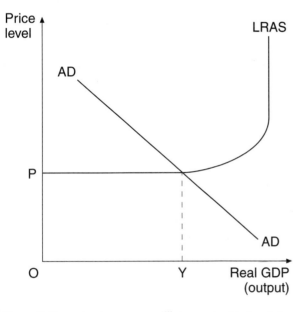

Figure 5 Keynesian long run equilibrium output below full employment

Quickies

- When is an economy not in equilibrium?
- What effect would an increase in aggregate demand be likely to have on the price level and output in the short run?
- Identify two causes of a fall in the price level.
- What does a vertical LRAS curve indicate?

Equilibrium level of real output (2)

As aggregate demand and aggregate supply are regularly changing, output and the price level are also frequently changing. This section examines how an economy can be in short run but not long run equilibrium, and how unexpected events can alter output and the price level.

Short run and long run equilibrium

Both Keynesian and new classical economists accept that it is possible for an economy to be in short run equilibrium but not necessarily in long run equilibrium. If, for example, aggregate demand rises to a very high level, in the short run domestic output may rise as a result of workers being prepared to work longer hours and low quality resources being used. In the longer run, the rise in costs that results will cause the short run aggregate supply curve to shift to the left and output to fall. Figure 1 uses the new classical version of the long run aggregate supply curve to illustrate this situation.

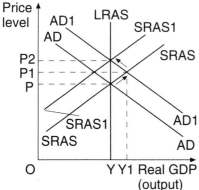

Figure 1 From short run to long run equilibrium

The economy is initially in short run and long run equilibrium at an output of Y. The increase in aggregate demand, illustrated by the shift in the aggregate demand curve from AD to AD1, causes output to rise in the short run. The economy moves to a new, higher-level, short run equilibrium output of Y1 and a higher equilibrium price level of P1. However, in the long run the higher costs that result from firms competing for increasingly scarce labour and raw materials, raises costs of production. The short run aggregate supply curve moves to the left to SRAS1. Firms realising that, in real terms with the price rises they gained being offset by higher costs, they are no better off so they reduce their output back to Y. The economy is now back to a position of both short run and long run equilibrium

Demand-side shocks

Demand-side shocks are unanticipated events that affect aggregate demand, shifting the AD curve and affecting the economy. These can be external or internal.

External shocks start in other countries. For example, in 1997 and 1998, a number of East Asian countries ran into significant difficulties, with some banks and other firms going out of business. The decline in economic activity reduced the demand for imports from Europe and the USA. As a result, Germany and the UK, among others, exported less to East Asia. This put downward pressure on their aggregate demand and reduced their rate of economic growth.

There can also be internal shocks. For example, households may become more optimistic about the future and as a result increase the amount they spend – a consumer boom.

Supply-side shocks

Supply-side shocks are again unanticipated events, but this time ones that affect aggregate supply. For example, if key groups of workers gain a pay rise, this may spread to other groups. Wage costs will rise, the short run aggregate supply curve will shift to the left and the price level will rise as shown on Figure 2.

Sudden changes in aggregate supply may also result from external events. If the price of oil increases, those countries that buy their oil from abroad will face higher costs of production.

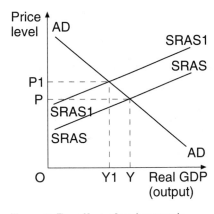

Figure 2 The effect of an increase in wage rates

Quickie

Illustrate the effect on UK real GDP and the price level of:

(a) a rise in demand for UK exports

(b) a rise in raw material costs

(c) advances in technology

(d) a cut in income tax.

Unemployment

3.12

A government seeks to achieve as low a level of unemployment as possible because of the costs that unemployment imposes. To be successful, it has to analyse the causes of any unemployment. In this spread you will consider the causes and consequences of unemployment.

Unemployment and employment

When the number and rate of people unemployed goes down, the number and rate of people employed usually increases, and vice versa. However, this does not have to occur and while, in practice, the figures usually move in opposite directions, they frequently do not move proportionately. For example, unemployment may fall by 30,000 one month, while employment rises by only 25,000. This situation occurs because there are a number of reasons why people cease to be unemployed, as shown in Figure 1. Unemployment increases whenever the inflow into unemployment exceeds the outflow from it.

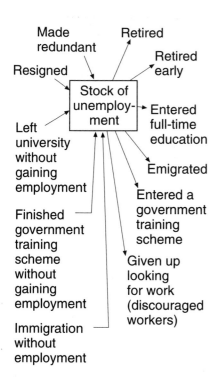

Figure 1 Inflows and outflows of unemployment

Duration of unemployment

As well as examining the number of people unemployed, the government is also concerned about how long people are out of work. This is because the longer people are out of work, the greater the costs involved. An unemployment rate of 6 per cent, with people on average being out of work for two years will create more problems than an unemployment rate of 9 per cent, with people being unemployed for an average of two months.

The causes of unemployment

Large-scale unemployment arises when aggregate demand is below the full employment level of aggregate supply. In this case, output is below the level that could be produced with all the labour force in work, as shown in Figure 2.

Over time, if aggregate demand grows more slowly than the increase in the productive capacity of the economy, there will be unemployment. Figure 3 illustrates AD growing more slowly than LRAS. There are a number of reasons why aggregate demand may rise more slowly or even fall. These include consumers becoming more pessimistic about the future and the country's products becoming less internationally competitive.

One cause of an increase in the country's productive capacity is an increase in the labour supply. If, for instance, more lone parents enter the labour force, the country will be capable of producing more goods and services.

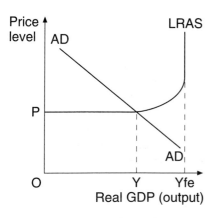

Figure 2 Output below the employment level

However, the effect a rise in the labour force has on employment and unemployment will depend on what is happening to aggregate demand and so the demand for labour.

Firms will also not want to employ people, even if aggregate demand is high and rising, if those people lack the appropriate skills and mobility.

The costs of unemployment

The main cost of unemployment to an economy is the **opportunity cost** of lost output – a potential output that is lost forever. When an economy has unemployed workers, it is not producing inside its production possibility frontier, at point *a*, as shown in Figure 4. With full employment it could produce at point *b*, *c* or any other point on the curve.

As well as lost output, there are a number of other costs that unemployment imposes on an economy. When people are out of work, they spend and earn less, so the government receives less revenue from indirect taxes such as VAT and from income tax.

While tax revenue will be less, government expenditure will have to be higher, as the government will have to spend more money providing Jobseeker's Allowance. If there was less unemployment, the government could spend more on other areas such as education or have lower tax rates. When people are out of work, they are more likely to suffer from poor physical and mental health. Financial worries and the loss of status can also contribute to mental ill-health, in some cases resulting in suicide or the breakdown of relationships. So unemployment can increase government expenditure on health services and supporting lone parents.

Of course, the people who bear the main burden of unemployment are the unemployed themselves. In addition, the longer people are unemployed, the more they miss out on training, updating and promotion and, as a result, the more difficult they will find it to gain employment once again.

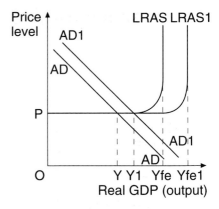

Figure 3 Aggregate demand growing more slowly than long run aggregate supply

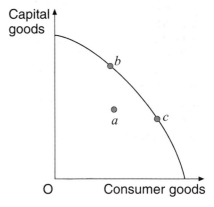

Figure 4 The opportunity costs of unemployment

Quickies

- What would explain a rise in unemployment being accompanied by a rise in unemployment?
- Why would improved training be expected to reduce unemployment?
- Use a production possibility frontier diagram to explain the effect of a reduction in unemployment on output.
- Why would a rise in employment be likely to raise government tax revenue?

Thinking like an economist

Discuss the effect that a rise in the school leaving age and a consumer boom is likely to have on unemployment.

Inflation

Price stability is another key economic objective. Prices are changing all the time, some rising and some falling. Inflation, though, is a sustained rise in the general (average) price level. So, if for example a fall in the price of personal computers is accompanied by a rise in the price of most other goods and services, the average change in price will be upwards and inflation will occur. When inflation takes place, the value of money will fall. Each unit of the currency, for example each pound, will be able to buy less than before.

The causes of inflation

There are thought to be two main causes of inflation. One is known as **demand-pull** inflation and the other is **cost-push** inflation.

Demand-pull inflation

Demand-pull inflation arises from aggregate demand increasing at a faster rate than aggregate supply. When the economy is producing at its productive capacity, increases in aggregate demand will pull up the price level, as shown in Figure 1, where Y is output.

Inflation can also occur when output is approaching its productive capacity. This is because as output rises, shortages of skilled workers and capital equipment begin to build up. Firms wanting to expand compete with each other for these scarce resources by bidding up their prices. So increases in aggregate demand can have an effect on costs of production. However, the starting point of the inflation is an excessive growth of aggregate demand.

Cost-push inflation

In contrast, the other main cause of inflation is increases in costs of production. This is a rise in the general cost level that arises independently of any change in aggregate demand.

A common cause of cost-push inflation is a rise in wage rates above increases in productivity. Such a rise increases costs of production. This can begin inflation as the higher wages are also likely to cause an increase in aggregate demand. This, in turn, may cause a rise in costs of production and so the process continues.

The effects of inflation

A high rate of inflation can cause many problems. During a period of **hyperinflation**, people usually lose confidence in the value of money and it can be difficult for an economy to operate. Even when inflation is not at hyperinflation but at levels that would be regarded as high, it can still impose costs on an economy. These include **menu**, **shoe leather** and

Figure 1 Demand-pull inflation

Definitions

Hyperinflation is a situation where the general price level is rising very rapidly and inflation is out of control.

Menu costs are the costs involved in changing prices due to inflation, e.g. in catalogues.

Shoe leather costs are the costs involved in moving money around in order to offset the effect of inflation.

administrative costs such as adjusting accounts and negotiating with unions about wage rises.

In addition, inflation creates a distortionary effect that is called **inflationary noise**. Without inflation, if the price of one model of television rises it can be concluded that it is relatively more expensive. However, with inflation consumers will be uncertain whether the rise in price reflects a relative price rise or whether it is just in line with inflation.

Unanticipated and anticipated inflation

Some costs can arise if the future inflation rate is not correctly anticipated. These costs may include people experiencing a fall in their real income. For example, if the rate of interest does not rise in line with inflation, the real rate of interest will fall and lenders will not be able to buy as much with the interest they receive. Some people, however, will gain from inflation. These include home buyers (since the value of property tends to rise by more than the rate of interest), other borrowers and workers with strong bargaining power. The government is also likely to gain from inflation. This is because it is usually a large net borrower, meaning it borrows a large amount, and if tax rates are not adjusted in line with inflation it may gain extra tax revenue – known as **fiscal drag**.

One of the most serious disadvantages of unanticipated inflation is the uncertainty it creates. For example, if firms are uncertain what their costs will be and what prices they will be able to gain, they may be reluctant to invest. This, in turn, will slow down economic growth.

However, when inflation is correctly anticipated, tax rates, pensions and wages can be adjusted in line with inflation.

Whether inflation is anticipated or not it can have a harmful effect on a country's international trade position. If the country's inflation rate is above that of its main competitors, its goods and services will become less price-competitive. This is likely to result in fewer exports being sold and more imports being purchased.

Definitions

Inflationary noise is the distortion of price signals (information) caused by inflation.

Fiscal drag is when inflation increases people's money income, dragging them into higher tax brackets.

Thinking like an economist

Explain why a stable inflation rate of 5 per cent persisting over 4 years will cause fewer problems than an inflation rate which fluctuates 2 two per cent to 8 per cent to 3 per cent to 7 per cent over the same period.

Research task

Using the *Economist* magazine, or any other appropriate source, compare the UK's inflation rate with that of the USA, France and Japan and consider the significance of the differences you find.

Quickies

- What is the difference between demand-pull and cost-push inflation?
- Why is unanticipated inflation likely to be more harmful than anticipated inflation?

Puzzler

Expectations of high inflation can cause high inflation to actually occur. Why do you think this is so?

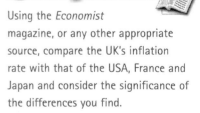

Balance of payments

The current account is a key part of the balance of payments. It consists of four sections:

- trade in goods
- trade in services
- investment income
- transfers.

Trade in goods

The UK often earns more from its exports of oil, chemicals and capital goods than it spends on imports. However, in many other categories, including consumer goods, food, beverages, tobacco and finished manufactured goods, it spends more on imports than it earns from exports. In recent years, the UK has had a deficit in trade in goods.

Trade in services

Services include travel (tourism), insurance, financial (banking) and computer and information services. The UK performs well in services. Since 1966, it has recorded a surplus every year. However, the surplus is usually smaller than the deficit on trade in goods, giving an overall trade gap.

Investment income

The UK usually has a surplus on investment income. This means that its residents earn more in terms of profits, interest and dividends on their assets held in other countries than foreigners earn on their investments in the UK.

Transfers

This covers transfers of money made and received by the government and individuals. These transfers include government payments to and from the EU, foreign aid payments, money sent to UK families by UK workers abroad and money sent out of the UK by foreigners working in the UK.

Thinking like an economist

Why might a fall in incomes in the USA have an adverse effect on the UK balance of payments?

The causes of a current account deficit

A deficit on the current account occurs when the country's expenditure abroad exceeds its revenue from abroad. In the UK's case, the most common reason for the current account to be **in the red** (overdrawn) is for there to be a deficit on the trade balance. That deficit may arise because the country is importing raw materials. This may be self-correcting as the raw materials may be converted into finished goods, some of which are exported.

It may also arise because the purchasers of the country's goods and services are experiencing economic difficulties and are not able to buy as many goods and services. When the economy improves, the deficit may disappear. In contrast, the domestic economy may be booming, and the high demand may suck in more imports and cause goods and services to be diverted from the export to the home market.

What is more serious is if the deficit is caused by a lack of price or quality competitiveness. In this case, the deficit will not be corrected without steps being taken to improve the performance of the country's firms.

The consequences of a current account deficit

The effects of a current account deficit will be influenced by its cause, its size and its duration. A small, self-correcting deficit is of less concern than one that is large and results from poor performance. When a country spends more than it earns, it is enjoying a higher living standard than it can afford. This may have to be financed by borrowing.

Exam hint

In assessing a current account deficit or surplus, remember to consider its causes, sizes and duration.

The causes of a current account surplus

A surplus on the current account is experienced when a country's revenue from abroad is greater than its expenditure abroad.

Care has to be taken in interpreting such a surplus. This is because it may arise from the strength or weakness of the economy. The country is likely to have a surplus if its products are very internationally competitive. However, it may also have a surplus if the country is in a recession. This is because its citizens will not be buying many products, including imports, and because its firms, finding it difficult to sell at home, may be competing more vigorously in the export market.

Making connections

Consider the effect of a rise in the country's inflation rate on its current account position.

The consequences of a current account surplus

A surplus will mean that more money is entering the country than leaving it and will make a positive contribution to aggregate demand. However, it may also involve more goods and services leaving the country than entering it.

Quickies

- What is meant by investment income?
- Which section of the current account is most commonly in deficit?

Economic growth

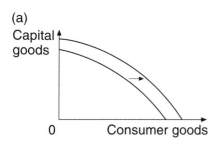

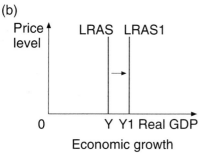

Figure 1 (a,b) Economic growth

Definitions

Productivity is output per worker hour.

Exam hint

Be careful when examining economic growth rates. For instance, in 2004 a country's economic growth rate may be 3 per cent and in 2005 it may be 2 per cent. This would mean that output is still rising but at a slower rate – but it is not falling.

Economic growth occurs when the productive capacity of the economy increases. It can be illustrated by a shift to the right of the production possibility frontier, as shown in Figure 1(a), or by a shift in the LRAS curve, as shown in Figure 1(b).

It is difficult to measure changes in productive capacity. So, as mentioned in Section 3.2, the main indicator of economic growth is taken to be the rate at which real GDP is changing.

Causes of economic growth

For economic growth to be achieved, there must be an increase in either the quantity and/or the quality of resources. For example, a country may be able to produce more, and therefore earn more, because it has more capital goods and/or because the capital goods it has are of a higher quality, incorporating advanced technological features.

The size and quality of the labour force may also increase. Among the possible causes of a rise in the size of the labour force are immigration, a rise in the retirement age and more lone parents entering the labour force. The two main causes of a rise in the quality of the labour force are improvements in education and training. A more educated and better-trained labour force will increase **productivity**.

Trend growth

In practice, the productive capacity of most economies increases each year. In industrialised economies this is due mainly to improvements in educational standards and advances in technology. In some developing economies it is also due to rises in the size of the labour force.

Trend growth is the expected increase in potential output over time and is a measure of how fast the economy can grow without generating higher inflation.

Causes of differences in countries' economic growth rates

Generally, rich economies grow at a more rapid rate than poor economies, although some developing economies are growing rapidly and are narrowing the gap between their real GDP per head and that of industrialised economies.

There are a number of reasons for the differences that exist between countries' economic growth rates. One is differences in expenditure on investment. Poor countries have low incomes, so their people are not able to save much. This reduces the funds and resources available for investment.

The resources devoted to education and training also differ. In poor countries very few people go on to higher education and in some countries, particularly in sub-Saharan Africa, the majority of children do not even receive secondary education.

Other reasons are thought to be differences in levels of international debt and changes in population size. A number of poor countries that have borrowed in the past in an attempt to improve their economic performance are now paying back more to rich countries in the form of interest payments than they are receiving in the form of foreign aid. This reduces their ability to spend money on investment, education and training. In some poor countries, a high birth rate also means that resources that could have been devoted to the production of capital goods and improved education have to be devoted to feeding, housing and educating the growing population.

Benefits and costs of economic growth

The main benefit of economic growth is likely to be a rise in people's material standard of living. If real GDP per head rises, the population can enjoy more products. Economic growth enables poverty to be reduced without having to redistribute existing income. Higher income also raises government tax revenue without having to increase tax rates. Some of this can be used to finance schemes to help the poor, improve public services (including education and health care) and improve the environment.

However, economic growth can also generate costs. In the short run, if the economy is operating at its productive capacity, there will be an opportunity cost in raising production. Some resources will have to be switched from making consumer goods to making capital goods. If economic growth is achieved in a way that is not sustainable – for instance, in a way that causes pollution – there will be damage to the environment. There is also the risk that economic growth may result in the depletion of non-renewable resources and increased stress caused by rapid change, resulting in negative externalities.

Hot potato

Do you think that an increase in the quantity of goods and services available to people always improves the quality of their lives?

Making connections

Explain why economic growth is a macroeconomic objective.

Quickies

- Identify two causes of economic growth.
- What is meant by trend growth?
- Why is it difficult for a poor country to invest?
- What is the main benefit of economic growth?

Puzzler

Why is the Chinese economy growing more rapidly than the UK's?

Inequality in income distribution

Definitions

Income is a flow of money over time.

Wealth is a stock of assets.

Thinking like an economist

Analyse the effect of an increase in university tuition fees on the distribution of income.

Figure 1 The 'haves' and 'have nots' of the UK in the twenty-first century

As well as trying to achieve price stability, full employment, a steady rate of economic growth and a satisfactory balance of payments, a government may seek to redistribute **income**.

The distribution of income in the UK

Households can receive income from employment (earned income), from investments in the form of dividends, interest and rent (unearned income) and from state benefits. Up until the last few years, the distribution of income between households was becoming more unequal.

There were a number of reasons for the widening of the gap between those with high incomes and those with low incomes which occurred in the 1980s and 1990s. One was the cut in top tax rates (see opposite) which, of course, benefited the rich most. Another was the rise in top executive pay that was sparked off initially by privatisation. At the other end of the income range, there was a decrease in the real value of benefits, particularly Jobseeker's Allowance, and a rise in the number of lone parents.

The causes of income inequality between households

There are a number of causes of differences in the incomes that households receive. One is the inequality in **wealth** distribution. As wealth generates income in the form of profit, interest and dividends, differentials in wealth generate differences in income (Figure 1).

Differences in the composition of households and employment also affect income distribution. Some households may have, say, three adults working, whereas other households may contain no one in employment. Low income is closely associated with dependency on benefits, whether through unemployment, disability or sickness.

Those with few or no skills are more likely to be out of work or in low-paid jobs. In contrast, those with high skills and qualifications are likely to be in high demand and so are likely to be able to earn high incomes. Earning capacity is influenced by differences in educational opportunities. The income of some groups in the UK is still adversely affected by discrimination in terms of employment opportunities, pay and promotion chances.

Among the other causes of inequality are differences in hours worked. Most full-time workers earn more than part-time workers and those who work overtime earn more than those who work standard hours.

The consequences of income inequality

Differences in earned income can provide incentives for workers to move from declining to expanding labour markets. Marked differences in income, however, may be considered to be unfair and lead to undesirable outcomes.

Poverty has a number of serious adverse effects on those who experience it. The poor tend to suffer worse physical and mental health and indeed have a lower life expectancy. The children of the poor suffer in terms of receiving less and often a lower quality of education. This can result in them gaining fewer qualifications and the development of a vicious circle of poverty developing. The poor can also feel cut off and even alienated from society, unable to live the type of life that the majority can experience.

Poverty can also impose costs on society. The poor place a large burden on state health care and are likely to be less productive, due to poorer health and fewer qualifications. Extremes in income can also give rise to social tensions.

Government policies

The government reduces income inequality on grounds of equity (fairness) and efficiency. In pursuit of this end, it uses a number of policy measures. One is progressive taxes, which take a higher percentage of the income or wealth of the rich. The government also provides cash benefits, such as housing benefit and benefits in kind (e.g. school meals), to help those on low incomes.

The government's labour market policy also influences income distribution. The National Minimum Wage introduced in 1999, anti-discrimination legislation and government subsidising of training reduce income inequality.

In addition, macroeconomic policy affects income distribution. For example, measures to reduce unemployment may benefit low-income households, and regional policy reduces geographical inequalities of income and wealth.

Hot potato

Would you favour an increase in income tax to finance increased unemployment benefits?

Quickies

- Identify two causes of income inequality.
- Explain one advantage of differences in earned income.
- Explain two costs to society of poverty.
- Identify two government policy measures that redistribute income.

Puzzler

How can the vicious circle of poverty be broken?

3.18 Monetary policy

Definitions

Monetary policy is government changes in the money supply, the rate of interest and the exchange rate.

Hot potato

The Monetary Policy Committee has been criticised for being too concerned with inflation. When deciding whether to change the rate of interest, some argue that more consideration should be given to the impact on employment and economic growth.

Making connections

Compare monetary policy and fiscal policy in terms of how they work and their effectiveness.

Research task

Each month, check on the MPC's decision on the rate of interest, what it has decided to do and why. This decision is usually announced in the middle of the month and good articles usually appear in the broadsheet papers. Also read the minutes of the monthly meetings of the MPC on the Bank of England's website.

Monetary policy measures include changes in the money supply, the rate of interest and the exchange rate. These measures are used by the government and its central bank to affect the economy by influencing aggregate demand and so, as with fiscal policies, are sometimes referred to as demand-side policies.

Changes in the money supply

An increase in the money supply is likely to increase aggregate demand. If the government prints more money or makes it easier for banks to lend more money, people will have more money to spend.

Changes in the rate of interest

The main monetary policy measure used is changes in the rate of interest. The Monetary Policy Committee (MPC) of the Bank of England sets its interest rate with the objective of keeping inflation close to the government's target level for RPIX of 2.5 per cent. If the MPC believes that aggregate demand is going to rise above the trend growth rate and so cause an increase in the inflation rate, it will raise the rate of interest. A higher rate of interest is likely to reduce consumption, investment and possibly net exports.

Household spending may fall as a result of savings receiving higher interest, borrowing becoming more expensive and mortgage borrowers having less money to spend after paying their now more expensive mortgage interest payments.

A higher rate of interest raises the cost of borrowing and the opportunity cost of using retained profits to finance investment. This higher cost and expectation of lower sales is likely to reduce investment.

A higher rate of interest may also encourage foreigners to buy the currency so that they can place money into the country's financial institutions and earn a high rate of return. Higher demand for the currency would raise its value. When the price of a currency increases, the country's exports rise in price and its imports fall in price. A change in prices of exports and imports may reduce export revenue and increase import expenditure and so lower net exports.

Changes in the exchange rate

As noted above, a change in the exchange rate affects aggregate demand by altering export and import prices. If a government wants to raise aggregate demand to reduce a deflationary gap (where AD is below the full employment level of AS), it may try to reduce the exchange rate. Such a reduction would increase the price competitiveness of the country's products and so increase exports and reduce imports, as shown in Figure 1. A government's central bank can reduce the value of its currency by lowering its interest rate or selling its currency.

The effectiveness of monetary policy

The main policy measure currently being used to influence short-term economic activity is changes in the rate of interest. This measure has the advantage that there is the opportunity to change it relatively quickly as the MPC meets every month. Changes in the exchange rate and the money supply, as well as in the interest rate, can have a significant impact on aggregate demand. However, it can take time for monetary policy measures to influence aggregate demand. For instance, it has been estimated that it can take eighteen months before a change in the rate of interest will alter consumption and investment plans.

In the 1970s and 1980s, it was found to be difficult to control the money supply, especially as banks have a strong profit motive to increase bank lending, and in the early 1990s the government found it difficult to maintain the value of the pound within set margins.

Monetary policy measures may have undesirable side-effects. A rise in the exchange rate, designed to reduce inflationary pressures, may worsen the balance of payments position and increase unemployment. Households and firms may also not react in the way expected. Lowering the rate of interest to stimulate rises in consumption and investment will not work if households and firms are pessimistic about future economic prospects.

The effects of monetary policy also tend to be more concentrated on certain groups than changes in income tax, for example, tend to be. For instance, a rise in the rate of interest will hit firms that export a high proportion of their output. This is because they will be affected not only by higher costs but also by a likely fall in demand resulting from a rise in the exchange rate.

In addition, a government's ability to change its interest rate is limited by the need for it to remain in line with other areas and countries' interest rates, most notably the EU's and the USA's, unless it is prepared to experience an inflow or outflow of portfolio investment funds.

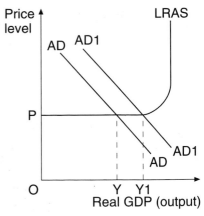

Figure 1 The effect of a reduction in the exchange rate

Figure 2 Mervyn King, Governor of the Bank of England

Exam hint

Most questions on monetary policy concentrate on interest rate changes.

Quickies

- What are the three instruments of monetary policy?
- Explain two reasons why a rise in the rate of interest is likely to reduce aggregate demand.
- What effect is a fall in the rate of interest likely to have on the exchange rate?
- Identify two limitations of monetary policy.

Supply-side policies

Supply-side policies, as the name suggests, seek to increase aggregate supply by increasing competition, productivity and flexibility in product and labour markets. The term covers a range of government policy measures, some of which are examined below.

Education and training

Improvements in education and training should raise productivity of labour. Output per worker hour will increase and the potential output of the economy will rise. This will shift the long run aggregate supply curve to the right, as shown in Figure 1.

Reduction in direct taxes

As well as increasing aggregate demand, lower direct taxation may also increase aggregate supply. This would be achieved by increasing incentives to firms, workers and potential workers. A cut in corporation tax will increase the funds that companies have available to invest, and so the subsequent return. If investment does increase, the productive capacity of the economy will rise.

Some economists believe that a cut in income tax will encourage some existing workers to work overtime, be more willing to accept promotion and to stay in the labour force for longer. In addition, they believe it will persuade more of the unemployed to accept employment at the going wage rate as their **disposable income** will rise. However, others argue that lower income tax rates may encourage some workers to take more leisure time as they can now gain the same disposable income by working fewer hours. It is also argued that what stops the unemployed from gaining employment is not a lack of willingness to work at the going wage rate, but a lack of jobs.

Reduction in unemployment benefit

Interventionist economists who believe that market failure is a significant problem and favour government intervention do not support a cut in Jobseeker's Allowance. They believe that what this will do is to reduce aggregate demand, output and employment.

However, supporters of free market forces argue that lowering Jobseeker's Allowance will, by widening the gap between employment and benefits, force the unemployed to seek work more actively and to accept employment at lower wage rates.

Reduction in trade union power

Those who favour the operation of free market forces believe that reductions in trade union power will reduce imperfections in the labour market. They argue that trade unions reduce employment by pushing wage rates above the

Key Term

Supply-side policies are policies designed to increase aggregate supply by raising the efficiency of markets.
Disposable income is the income available after direct taxation has been deducted and state benefits have been added.

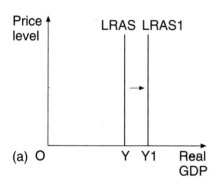

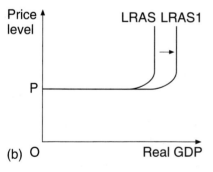

Figure 1 (a,b) The result of improvements in education and training

equilibrium level and by encouraging workers to engage in restrictive practices. These economists suggest that reducing the power of trade unions will increase labour productivity and reduce the cost of employing labour. As a result, firms will be encouraged to employ more workers and raise output.

Again, some economists disagree. They argue that trade unions act as a counter-balance to the market imperfection of very powerful employers. They also claim they reduce firms' costs by acting as a channel for communication between employers and workers, as it is cheaper to negotiate with one body than with individual workers.

Privatisation and deregulation

Supporters of free market forces argue that government intervention in the economy should be reduced. They believe that firms are in the best position to make decisions about what to produce, how to produce and what to charge. This is because they are subject to the discipline of the market. If they do not provide the products that consumers want at competitive prices, it is argued, they will go out of business. So these economists favour the deregulation of firms and the transfer of firms from the public to the private sector.

However, some argue that rules, regulations and/or government ownership of firms are beneficial in a number of circumstances where there is a high risk of market failure.

can only be done once

The effectiveness of supply-side policies

Supply-side policies are now widely used by governments. They have the advantage that they are selective, targeted at particular markets and are designed to raise efficiency and help the government to achieve its objectives. Increasing aggregate supply enables aggregate demand to continue to rise over time without inflationary pressures building up. A higher quality of resources should also make domestic firms more price and quality competitive and so improve the country's balance of payments position.

However, as noted above, there is disagreement about whether a **free market** or **interventionist** approach should be adopted, with differences of opinion about, for instance, how potential workers respond to cuts in benefits and whether firms operate more efficiently in the public or private sector. Some of the policies, such as education spending, also take a relatively long time to have an effect.

Hot potatoes

What do you think is the best way of encouraging lone parents to enter the labour force?

Why may a cut in income tax rates have no effect on the number of hours people work?

Quickies ✓

- What is meant by deregulation?
- Identify one strength and one limitation of supply-side policies.

Policies to reduce unemployment

There is a range of policies a government may employ to reduce unemployment. The choice of measures will be influenced by the cause of unemployment, the rate and duration of unemployment and the state of the other key macroeconomic objectives. In the short run, unemployment may be reduced by measures that increase aggregate demand but in the long run, supply-side measures are likely to be more effective.

Short run

In the short run, with an economy operating below its productive capacity, unemployment may be reduced by increases in aggregate demand. Expansionary fiscal and monetary policy can be used to create jobs. A government could increase its spending and/or cut tax rates in order to raise aggregate demand. In practice, a rise in government spending has the potential to have more of an impact on aggregate demand, and so unemployment, than cuts in taxes. This is because some of the rise in disposable income that results from lower taxes may be saved and some spent on imports and so not increase aggregate demand.

Increases in the money supply and lower interest rates are also likely to raise aggregate demand. For instance, a fall in interest rates and/or an increase in the money supply should stimulate consumption and investment. It may also raise net exports if it causes a fall in the exchange rate. Figure 1 shows the effect of a rise in aggregate demand on real GDP.

Expansionary fiscal and monetary policies may have undesirable side-effects. One consequence of a rise in aggregate demand may be a rise in the price level as the economy approaches the full employment level. The higher level of spending may also increase any existing deficit on the current account of the balance of payments.

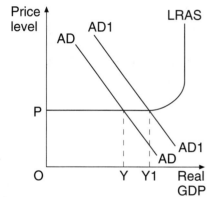

Figure 1 The effect of an increase in aggregate demand

Long run

In the long run, if there is not a shortage of aggregate demand, the cause of unemployment will lie with supply-side problems. Those people who are out of work when the level of demand is high and there is no shortage of job vacancies are likely to be between jobs, lacking the appropriate skills, geographically or occupationally immobile, have family circumstances that restrict their ability to work or are lacking the incentive to move off benefits and find employment.

There are a number of factors that determine such unemployment. The time people spend finding a job after they have left another job is influenced by the quantity of information they have about job vacancies. Many of the long-term unemployed lack qualifications, have poor communication skills and are geographically immobile. Some may have lost the work habit, have difficulties affording child care, find problems with overcoming prejudice about them working (e.g. the disabled) and some may believe they are better off on benefits than in employment.

In these circumstances, it is unlikely that raising aggregate demand will succeed in reducing unemployment. What is needed is an increase in the attractiveness of work to the unemployed and an increase in the attractiveness of the unemployed to employers. Supply-side policies are likely to be more effective in achieving these objectives than demand-side policies.

Supply-side polices

Supply-side policies can be implemented to increase economic incentives and the quality of the labour services offered by the unemployed. Such measures include the provision of information, improved education and training, the provision of work experience, financial support for child care, and a widening of the gap between the income received from employment and the income received in benefits. The latter measure can include, for instance, a reduction in the **marginal tax rate**.

The New Deal

The need to tackle the problems of long-term unemployment and youth unemployment lay behind the introduction of the New Deal by the Labour government in 1998. This scheme provided help and advice to the unemployed in seeking a job during the first four months of unemployment. After this period, the unemployed have four options. They can take up the offer of a job subsidised by the government, take a place on an educational or training course, undertake voluntary work or work with an environmental task force. The intention behind these options is to develop skills, confidence and work experience.

Unemployment and the full employment level

When the unemployment percentage is coming close to the full employment level, it becomes increasingly difficult to reduce unemployment further. If, however, policy measures succeed in reducing the time people spend between jobs and in long-term unemployment, the unemployment percentage at the full employment level may possibly be reduced.

Web link

Look at the website of the Institute of Fiscal Studies by going to www.heinemann.co.uk/hotlinks and entering express code 0829P.

Definition

Marginal tax rate is the proportion of extra income that is taken in tax.

Making connections

Discuss the benefits that would be experienced as a result of a fall in unemployment.

Quickies

- Identify two policy measures a government could implement to increase aggregate demand.
- Explain two reasons why someone may be unemployed.

3.21

Policies to control inflation

f a country is experiencing inflation, the measures it implements will be influenced by what is thought to be causing the inflation. As well as tackling any current inflation, governments also implement measures they hope will ensure long run price stability.

Short run

There are a number of policy measures a government can take to control inflation in the short run.

Cost-push inflation

If a government believes that inflation is caused by excessive increases in wage rates, it may try to restrict wage rises. It can control wages in the public sector by restricting increases in government spending allocated to public sector wage rises. It can also restrict wage rises in both the public and private sectors by introducing an **incomes policy**. This measure does seek to reduce inflation without causing unemployment. However, in practice, a number of problems arise with the operation of incomes policies. These include the fact that employers and employees often find ways around the limit.

A limit on wage rises also introduces a degree of inflexibility in labour markets. Firms wanting to expand and attract more labour will be unable to raise wages as much as they would like. These and other problems have discouraged UK and many other governments using incomes policies in recent decades.

Demand-pull inflation

To reduce demand-pull inflation a government may adopt deflationary fiscal and/or monetary policy measures. These are ones that seek to reduce inflation by decreasing aggregate demand, or at least the growth of aggregate demand. A government could, for instance, raise income tax. This would reduce people's disposable income and their ability to spend.

The main short-run anti-inflationary measure being employed in the UK, however, is currently changes in interest rates. Higher interest rates are likely to reduce aggregate demand by reducing consumption, investment and possibly net exports.

The Monetary Policy Committee

The Monetary Policy Committee (MPC) of the Bank of England sets the rate of interest with the main objective of achieving the government's target rate of inflation of 2.5 per cent, as measured by the RPIX. Subject to meeting that objective, it has been instructed to support the economic policy of the government, including its objectives for employment and economic growth. The MPC consists of five members drawn from employees of the Bank of

Definition

Incomes policy is a limit on wage increases.

Web links

Find out more about the Bank of England by going to: www.heinemann.co.uk/hotlinks and entering express code 0829P.

England, including the Governor of the Bank of England, and four economists nominated by the Chancellor of the Exchequer. It meets monthly to review evidence on the performance of the economy and indicators of changes in inflationary pressure. This information includes figures on the current and predicted growth of the money supply, the exchange rate, wage rates, employment, productivity, retail sales and surveys of business and consumer confidence. If the MPC believes that the information points to a risk that inflation will rise above the target, it will raise its interest rate.

Monetary policy stance

A tight (or restrictionist) monetary policy is one that aims to reduce aggregate demand, or at least the growth of aggregate demand, usually in a bid to lower inflation or improve the balance of payments position. In contrast, an expansionary monetary policy approach (loose monetary policy) is one that seeks to stimulate a growth in aggregate demand. So reducing the rate of interest would be regarded as an expansionary approach.

Longrun

In the long run, a government is likely to seek to reduce the possibility of inflationary pressure by increasing long run aggregate supply. If the productive capacity of the economy grows in line with aggregate demand, with shifts in the AD curve being matched by shifts in the LRAS curve, the economy can grow without the price level rising. This will enable people to enjoy more goods and services without the economy experiencing inflationary and balance of payments problems.

As noted in Section 3.21, the policies used to increase long run aggregate supply are supply-side policies. Those are, of course, a long-run approach to controlling inflationary pressure as they take time to have their full impact on productive capacity. However, they do have the advantage that they do not have the adverse short-run side-effects on employment and output that deflationary fiscal and monetary policy may pose.

Quickies

- What is meant by deflationary fiscal policy?
- Explain a possible disadvantage of deflationary monetary policy.

Puzzler

Explain three reasons that may lead the MPC to believe that the inflation rate will rise in the future.

3.22

Policies to improve the balance of payments

As with other objectives, there are both short-run and long-run policy measures that a government can use to improve its balance of payments position. Again, the short-run measures tend to concentrate on demand while the long-run measures focus on improving the supply-side performance of the economy.

Short run

In the short run, there are three main policy measures a government can seek to raise export revenue and/or reduce import expenditure in the case of a current account deficit. These are for the government to reduce the value of the currency, to reduce domestic spending and to increase import restrictions. Each measure has the potential to improve the balance of payments position but also has its limitations.

Exchange rate adjustment

A country may seek to reduce its exchange rate if it believes that its current level is too high and as a result is causing its products to be uncompetitive against rival countries' products. **A depreciation** will cause export prices to fall in terms of foreign countries' currencies, and cause import prices to rise in terms of the domestic currency.

However, to succeed in increasing export revenue and reducing import expenditure it is important that demand for exports and imports is price elastic, that other countries do not devalue and do not increase their import restrictions.

If the fall in the exchange rate increases demand for the country's products, it is likely that employment and output will also rise in the short run. However, by increasing demand for the country's products and raising import prices, it may lead to inflationary pressures.

Demand management

To discourage expenditure on imports and to encourage some products to be switched from the home to the export market, a government may adopt deflationary fiscal and monetary policy measures. Domestic spending may be reduced by higher taxation, lower government spending and/or higher interest rates. However, there is the risk that the resulting reduction in spending may cause output to fall and unemployment to rise.

Import restrictions

A country may seek to reduce expenditure on imports by imposing import restrictions including **tariffs** and **quotas**. However, such measures may have inflationary side effects. For example, imposing tariffs will increase the price of some products bought in the country, raise the cost of imported raw materials and reduce competitive pressure on domestic firms to keep costs and prices low.

Making connections

Explain how a government could seek to reduce the value of its currency.

Definition

Depreciation is a fall in the value of the currency.

A tariff is a tax on imports.

A quota is a limit on imports.

Placing restrictions on imports also runs the risk of provoking retaliation. In addition, membership of a trade bloc such as the EU and of the **World Trade Organization (WTO)** limits the independent action that a country can take on import restrictions.

Long run

If a deficit arises from a lack of quality competitiveness, lower labour productivity or higher inflationary pressure, then reducing the value of the currency, deflationary policy measures and import restrictions will not provide long-term solutions. In such a situation, the most appropriate approach would be to implement supply-side policies.

Supply-side policies

To raise international competitiveness, there are a number of supply-side policies a government may take, including:

- cutting corporation tax to stimulate investment
- cutting income tax to encourage enterprise and effort
- privatising industries if it is thought that firms will operate more efficiently in the private sector
- deregulating markets to promote competition
- promoting education and training to increase productivity and reduce labour costs.

How successful these measures are depends on the appropriateness of the measures, i.e. the type of training provided, and how firms and workers respond to the incentives provided. The measures can also take a relatively long time to have an effect.

Current account surplus

A balance of payments disequilibrium may also arise because of a current account surplus. A government may seek to reduce or remove a surplus in order to avoid inflationary pressures and to raise the amount of imports it can enjoy. To reduce a surplus a government may seek to raise the value of its currency, introduce reflationary fiscal and monetary policy measures and/or reduce import restrictions.

Definitions

The World Trade Organization (WTO) is an international organisation that promotes free international trade and rules on international trade disputes.

Web link

Find out more about the World Trade Organisation by visiting www.heinemann.co.uk/hotlinks and entering express code 0829P.

Quickies ✓

- Identify two factors that will influence the success of a depreciation in improving the balance of payments.
- Explain a disadvantage of import restrictions.
- Identify two possible causes of a current account deficit.
- Why may a government seek to reduce a current account surplus?

Policies to promote economic growth

In this spread you will examine policy measures a government may use to increase output in the short run, and the long run measures that can be implemented to increase economic growth. You will also examine why governments seek to achieve stable economic growth and the nature of business cycles.

Short run

Increases in output in the short run can occur due to increases in aggregate demand if the economy is initially producing below its productive capacity. In a situation of low economic activity, aggregate demand may be stimulated by expansionary fiscal and/or monetary policy. Some measures of fiscal and monetary policies have the advantage that they may increase both aggregate demand and, in the long run, aggregate supply. For instance, a lower rate of interest is likely to stimulate consumption but also investment and higher investment will raise long run aggregate supply. Increases in some forms of government spending – for example, spending on education and research and development – will also shift the long run aggregate supply curve to the right.

Long run

In the long run, increases in output can continue to be achieved only if the productive capacity of the economy increases. This is why changes in long run aggregate supply are so important. So, for economic growth to occur the quality and/or quantity of resources have to increase. Supply-side policies seek to achieve such an outcome. For instance, measures that raise investment will increase long run aggregate supply. The extent of the increase will depend on the amount of investment, its type and how efficiently it is used. Capital deepening will be more effective than capital widening. Capital deepening involves increasing the amount of capital per worker. This should raise labour productivity. Capital widening occurs when investment increases to keep up with increases in the supply of labour.

To use capital efficiently, it is important to have educated and healthy workers. Investment in human capital should increase the productive capacity of the economy, but again the extent to which this occurs is influenced by the appropriateness and the quality of the investment. For example, the function of training and one of the functions of education should be to develop the skills needed in the competitive world market. These include not only numeracy and literacy but also communication, interpersonal skills and literacy and computer technology skills. While the increases in the quality and quantity of training and secondary education in a number of countries, including the newly industrialised countries, have come in for praise, the UK has been criticised for its low levels of training, educational standards and staying-on rates.

Exam hint

Emphasise the importance of supply-side policies in improving the potential capacity of the economy.

Making connections

Discuss four supply-side policies that could be implemented to promote economic growth.

Stable growth

In seeking to promote economic growth, most governments aim for stable growth. Their objective is for actual growth to match trend growth and for trend growth (see section 3.16) to rise over time.

Governments try to avoid aggregate demand increasing faster than the trend growth rate permits, since this can result in the economy overheating, with inflation and balance of payments difficulties arising. They also try to stop aggregate demand rising more slowly than the trend growth rate, since this would mean an output gap developing, with unemployed resources.

The Labour government, when first elected in 1997, gave as one of its objectives the end of 'boom and bust'. One way the Labour government has sought to achieve greater economic stability is by creating stability of economic policy. It has, for instance, given the Bank of England independence to determine interest rates (subject to its need to meet the government's inflation target), sets three-year spending plans for government departments and has put limits on the level of government debt.

Effects of business cycles

Business cycles, which are sometimes referred to as trade cycles, describe the tendency for economic activity to fluctuate outside its trend growth rate, moving from a high level of economic activity (boom) to negative economic growth (recession/bust). Governments seek to dampen down these cyclical fluctuations because of the harmful effects they can have on the performance of the economy. When it is uncertain that aggregate demand will continue to rise, this will tend to discourage investment. It may also mean that firms are reluctant to increase employment opportunities. During an upturn, some employers may be reluctant to take on more workers for fear that the increased level of activity will not last, while during a downturn, some may hoard labour.

Quickies

- Why are supply-side policies so important in promoting economic growth?
- Distinguish between an economic boom and a recession.

Key concept

Remember that the total level of national income is calculated in the same way as aggregate demand under the expenditure method of calculation. Since we are only trying to find the total value of output of UK goods and services, the level of consumption of foreign goods must be removed to avoid double counting.

Activity 1

Calculate the level of the UK national income in 2001 based on the following:

Total final consumption = £630 billion
Government spending = £217 billion
Investment = £164 billion
Exports = £268 billion
Imports = £290 billion

What was the level of net exports?

Activity 2

(a) Define what is meant by economic growth and the economic standard of living.
(b) What are three benefits and three problems associated with a rapid rate of economic growth?
(c) Identify three problems an economist might face when attempting to compare the standard of living in different nations, using real national income per capita data.

Activity 3

The underlying rate of inflation, RPIX, jumped from 2.7 per cent to 3 per cent in February 2003, while the headline RPI rate rose from 2.9 per cent in January to 3.2 per cent. Underlying inflation has now been above the Bank of England's target for four months, prompting speculation about the possibility of an increase in interest rates. Most analysts expect inflation to peak in June given that it hit its lowest level last June, bottoming out at 1.5 per cent, the lowest level possible without the MPC having to write an open letter of explanation to the Chancellor. Economists had expected petrol prices to play a large part in the increase in retail prices but the biggest influence proved to be higher clothing prices, as shops marked up their goods after the January sales. Price increases in fresh vegetables – including cucumbers and lettuces – also contributed to the higher-than-expected figure. February's figures were based on a revised basket of goods being used to calculate inflation. The new selection of goods and services includes takeaway latte coffees, golf green fees, and powdered diet drinks, while brown ale, tinned spaghetti and vinyl flooring have all been dropped.

Adapted from the BBC news website.

(a) Distinguish between the RPI and RPIX measures of inflation.

(b) In what circumstances is it likely that the RPIX is higher than the RPI?

(c) Why might economists believe that inflation would peak in June?

(d) Using examples from the passage explain what is meant by a 'weighted' index.

(e) Identify four significant costs of inflation.

Activity 4

Using aggregate demand and aggregate supply analysis, explain the effect of each of the following on the equilibrium level of real output in the UK.

(a) A decrease in the value of the pound against the euro.

(b) An increase in the basic rate of income tax.

(c) An improvement in business confidence that leads to a substantial increase in business investment in the UK.

Activity 5

(a) What is meant by the 'unemployment rate?'

(b) Distinguish between the Claimant count and the Labour Force Survey methods of calculating the level of unemployment.

(c) Assess the effectiveness of supply-side policies to reduce the level of unemployment.

Exam hints

It is vital that you try to incorporate AD/AS diagrams into your analysis in Unit 3. Label the axes correctly and make links to the diagram in your answer. You must be confident in distinguishing between the causes of an AD and AS shift.

Boost your grade

Note the keyword 'assess' in part (c) of Question in Activity 5. This means that the answer requires some evaluation. You should consider the relative strengths of your arguments, look at a counterpoint, consider the short and long-run implications and come to some overall conclusion to your analysis.

Activity 1

UK national income (GDP) by the expenditure method is:

C (£630 bn) + I (£164 bn) + G (£217 bn) + (X (£268 bn) – M (£290 bn)) = £989 bn.

Net exports (X – M) were –£22 billion.

Activity 2

(a) Economic growth is the rate of increase of the total value of our economy's output, normally measured per annum. It is normally expressed as the percentage change in real GDP. The economic standard of living is most commonly measured using the real GDP per capita (per head of the population).

(b) A rapid rate of growth may lead to:
- Fast growth of real incomes of individuals, leading to a rapid reduction in the numbers of people in poverty.
- It may create a large number of jobs that will help to reduce unemployment rates.
- It may lead to a large increase in the amount of tax collected from **direct taxes**, helping to provide funds to improve the quality of public services.

However growth may also have some disadvantages:
- It may lead to negative externalities from all the additional production that may damage the environment.
- It might require people to work much longer hours so that although they may be materially better off, their standards of living may have got worse due to a lack of leisure time.
- Fast growth may lead to a large increase in the volume of imports that we purchase, producing trade deficit problems.

(c)
- Different nations may have differently-sized informal economies and black markets.
- Different economies have very different distributions of income.
- A common currency must be used, but market exchange rates may not reflect the true differences in the purchasing power of those currencies in their own nation.

Activity 3

(a) The RPIX excludes the effects of changes in mortgage interest repayments on the headline RPI rate of inflation.

(b) If mortgage interest costs have been falling due to reductions in interest rates then this will be reflected in falling costs of living in the RPI, but it

Definitions

Direct taxes are those taken directly from sources of income, such as income tax, national insurance contributions and corporation tax. They differ from indirect taxes, which are levied on the expenditure of consumers, such as VAT.

will not help to reduce the RPIX rate of inflation. Therefore the RPI rate of average price rise will be slower than the RPIX rate.

(c) The RPI is measured on a year-on-year basis. That is, prices this June are compared to the prices last June (and not the previous month). Since prices had their lowest rate of increase last June it is likely that they have risen substantially since.

(d) The 'weighted' RPI gives more importance to the change in prices of those goods or services that affect our costs of living the most. Thus as brown ale and vinyl flooring have become less widely consumed, their weight has diminished to the point where they are no longer being including in the RPI basket of goods being monitored.

(e) Menu costs, shoe leather costs, industrial relations difficulties in wage bargaining, delays in investment plans due to uncertainty.

Activity 4

(a) This is likely to increase AD, as it will reduce the price of exports in foreign currency and increase the price of imported goods in sterling.

(b) This will cause a reduction in AD, as it reduces the disposable income available for consumption. It may also lead to a smaller multiplier effect from any injection. There may also be a reduction in AS if individual's work incentives are severely affected by a rise in income tax.

(c) Investment will cause AD to shift to the right. It will also stimulate a multiplier increase in AD due to the additional incomes and consumption that it generates. The AS will shift to the right in the long run as UK firms will be capable of producing more.

Activity 5

(a) The unemployed as a percentage of the workforce.

(b) *See* the Definitions (*right*).

(c) Show how supply-side policies shift the AS to the right, raising output and creating employment. They may also reduce inflationary pressure. Give some examples of supply-side policies to reduce unemployment, or to raise productivity and growth. Evaluate, by showing how aggregate demand is also needed to create jobs. Skilled and motivated unemployed people will not get a job without job vacancies in the economy.

Definitions

Claimant count = all unemployed, eligible for and actually claiming Jobseeker's Allowance.

Labour Force Survey = a 3-monthly survey of people who have sought work in the last 4 weeks and can start in the next 2 weeks, or who are waiting to start work in the next 2 weeks.

3.26 Exam guidance and practice

Unit 3: Managing the economy

Unit 3 is an hour-long paper consisting of one data-response from a choice of two. Each data-response is split into seven parts and one part will require extended prose. Therefore, where there previously would have been an essay question, this has now been incorporated into part of a data-response that will require you to write at some length, using your retained knowledge of macroeconomic theory as well as the provided passage for stimulus. It is likely that the extended question will have some evaluative content, so watch out for the keywords, 'assess', 'evaluate' or 'to what extent'.

- Assess the relative importance of the point that you are making.
- Are there time-lag effects? What will be the short-and long-run effects?
- Can you make a counterpoint that would be relevant to the point you have just made?
- Draw your argument to some overall conclusion. Remember that the quantity of supporting arguments behind a case is not the decisive factor. It is the strength of the argument that is crucial.

As with Units 1 and 2, it is very important that you spend the first 5–10 minutes reading carefully through the data-responses to choose the correct one. Read the questions first, concentrating on whether you can give a good answer to the later questions that are worth more marks. Allocate your time in proportion to the number of marks that the question has. Make sure that you do not spend too long on preliminary questions that are not worth that many marks.

The data-response passages are drawn from real-world information, so a working knowledge of what has occurred to the UK economy and why, at least since the last recession in 1990–91, can be very helpful. Concentrate on the five main macroeconomic objectives in your revision. What policies have been used and how effective have they been?

Sample question

The UK trade deficit hit £3.98 billion in November 2002, the worst monthly figure since records began in 1697. Traditionally Britain runs a deficit in its trade in goods, but that is balanced by extra income from trade in services (like insurance, shipping and music royalties) and investments overseas. However, the trade deficit has been getting worse in recent months, as UK consumers buy more goods made overseas. This has, in part, been a symptom of the higher growth of the UK economy than our major trading partners. UK exports overseas have been hit by the high value of the pound, which has made them more expensive, and also hit by the slowdown in our main export markets in the United States and Europe.

(a) What is meant by a trade deficit?

(b) What is a current account deficit?

(c) Is a current account deficit a sign of economic strength or a symptom of economic weakness?

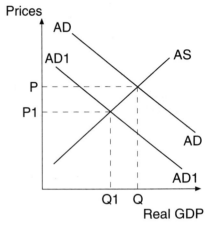

Figure 1

Answers

(a) The trade deficit is a misleading term as it refers only to the trade in goods, or what used to be referred to as the visible balance. It means that the value of goods exported from the UK to other countries was exceeded by the value of goods that the UK imported.

(b) The current account of the balance of payments measures the trade balance, the balance of trade in services, investment income flows and transfers between the UK and other nations. A current account deficit implies that more money flowed out of the UK than into the UK for these purposes

(c) The passage indicates that you could view a current account deficit as a symptom of the relative strength of economic growth in our economy compared to our trading partners. As our GDP and incomes grow faster this year than their economies, our demand for their imports may grow faster than their demand for our exports. A current account deficit may also be a useful deflationary device, holding back our aggregate demand at a time when the domestic economy finds it difficult to meet that level.

However, the current account deficit could instead be a sign of poor competitiveness of UK goods and services, or of the lack of a strong UK manufacturing industry capable of meeting our own demands. The deficit would reduce AD, since AD = C + I + G + (X – M), and this may cause a reduction in output and employment in the UK, as illustrated in Figure 1.

Further reading

3.2
C. Bamford & S.Grant, *The UK Economy in a Global Context*, 2000, Chapter 2

3.33
C. Bamford & S. Grant, *The UK Economy in a Global Context*, 2000, Chapter 2.
S.Grant, *Economic Growth and Business Cycles*, 1999, Chapter 4.
M. Russell and D. Heathfield, *UK Monetary Policy*, 1999, Chapter 2.

3.4
C. Bamford & S. Grant, *The UK Economy in a Global Economy*, 2000, Chapter 2

3.6
C. Bamford & S. Grant, *The UK Economy in a Global Context*, 2000, Chapter 1

3.7
C. Bamford & S. Grant, *UK Economy in a Global Context*, 2000, Chapter 1

3.8
C. Bamford & S. Grant, *UK Economy in a Global Context*, 2000, Chapter 1

3.9
C. Bamford & S. Grant, *The UK Economy,* 2000, Chapter 1

3.10
C. Bamford & S. Grant, *The UK Economy,* 2000, Chapter 1

3.11
C. Bamford & S. Grant, *The UK Economy*, 2000, Chapter 1

3.13
C. Bamford & S. Grant, *The UK Economy in a Global Context*, 2000, Chapter 6
G. Hale, *Labour Markets*, 2001, Chapter 5
D. Smith, *UK Current Economic Policy*, 2nd edition, 1999, Chapter 5

3.14
M. Russell & D. Heathfield, *Inflation and UK Monetary Policy*, 1999,
    Chapters 1–5
C. Bamford & S. Grant, *The UK Economy in a Global Context*, 2000,
    Chapter 6

3.15

C. Bamford & S. Grant, *The UK Economy in Global Context*, 2000, Chapter 2

3.16

C. Bamford & S. Grant, *The UK Economy in a Global Context*, 2000, Chapter 7
S. Grant, *Economic Growth and Business Cycles*, 1999, Chapters 1–6

3.17

G. Hale, *Labour Markets*, 2001, Chapters 6 and 7

3.19

David Smith, *UK Current Economic Policy*, 2003, Chapters 3 and 4

3.20

Mark Russell & David Heathfield, *Inflation and UK Monetary Policy*, 1999,
Chapters 6–9

3.21

C. Bamford & S. Grant, *The UK Economy in a Global Context*, 2000, Chapter 3
M. Cook & N. Healey, *Supply-side Policies, 4th edition*, 2001, Chapters 3–7
D. Smith, *UK Current Economic Policy, 2nd edition*, 2003, Chapter 2

3.22

C. Bamford & S. Grant, *The UK Economy in a Global Context*, 2000, Chapter 3

3.23

David Smith, *UK Current Economic Policy, 2nd edition*, 2003, Chapter 4
M.Russell & D.Heathfield, *Inflation and UK Monetary Policy, 3rd edition*,
    1999, Chapter 8
C. Bamford & S. Grant, *The UK Economy in a Global Context*, 2000,
    Chapter 6

3.24

C. Bamford & S. Grant, *The UK Economy in a Global Context*, 2000, Chapter 4

3.25

D.Smith, *UK Current Economic Policy, 2nd edition*, 2003, Chapter 6
C. Bamford & S. Grant, *The UK Economy in a Global Context*, 2000, Chapter 7
S. Grant, *Economic Growth and Business Cycles*, 1999, Chapters 2–4

Glossary

Aggregate demand	The total demand for a country's goods and services at a given price level.
Aggregate supply	The total output of a country's producers supply at a given price level.
Allocative efficiency	Refers to who gets what. An economy would be allocatively efficient if everybody received exactly those goods and services for which they were prepared to pay the market price.
Balance of payments	A record of transactions between a country's residents and the rest of the world.
Barter	Where one group of people with a surplus of something, say, fish, swaps with another group able to produce, say, more grain.
Brand loyalty	A term often used in business to explain why customers stick to the same brand.
Buffer stocks	Stocks held by a government to smooth out changes in prices by the sale and purchase of stocks.
Business cycles	Fluctuations in economic activity over time, often referred to as booms and busts.
Capital goods	Goods that are used to produce other goods and services
Ceteris paribus	Others things considered equal.
Circular flow of income	A model involving flows of income and goods meant to illustrate the way spending and incomes move around the economy.
Claimant count	A measure of unemployment that includes those recieving Jobseeker's Allowance.
Complements	Goods which are used together.
Consumption	The proportion of a households' income spent on goods and services.

Cost benefit analysis	Calculations involving social costs and benefits, used to assess the viability of both private and public investments or projects.
Cost-push inflation	A rise in the price level caused by increases in the costs of production.
Cross elasticity of demand	The elasticity of demand for one good in relation to changes in the price of another.
Degradation	The effects of pollution spoiling the quality of all available resources.
Demand curve	Shows the likely relationship between the price of a good or service and the quantity sold. These curves usually slope downwards from left to right, showing either that as price falls, demand is likely to rise, or that as price rises, demand is likely to fall.
Demand-pull inflation	A rise in the price level caused by increases in aggregate demand.
Demerit good	Goods that are considered to be socially undesirable.
Depletion	The using up of non-renewable resources.
Depreciation	A fall in the value of currency.
Deregulation	The removal of government restrictions and controls on business activity.
Direct tax	Tax on the income of individuals and firms.
Disposable income	Income after direct taxation has been deducted and state benefits have been added.
Division of labour	Breaking up the production process into individual jobs.
Economies of scale	Factors which contribute to decreasing long-run average costs.
Elastic	Responsive.

Equilibrium	When two forces are equal. Often refers to demand and supply.
Excess supply	Situation in which supply exceeds demand.
Externalities	Occur when there is a divergence between private and social costs and/or between private and social benefits.
Factor immobility	A situation in which factors of production do not move readily in responses to changes in their price.
Factor markets	Intermediate markets in which the factors of production are traded.
Factors of production	Land, labour, capital and enterprise which are used in varying proportions to produce goods and services.
Fiscal drag	When inflation increases people's money incomes, dragging them into higher tax brackets.
Fiscal policy	Changes in government spending and taxation.
Free market approach	Leaving markets to work without government or other external intervention.
Full employment	A situation where those wanting to work can gain employment at the going wage rate – often taken as an unemployment rate of 3 per cent.
Globalisation	The broadening of markets and production to a world-wide scale.
Government administrations	Government regimes that run the length of a parliament, e.g. the Labour Government 1997–2001.
Gross Domestic Product	Total output of the economy.
Human capital	Education, training and experience that a worker possesses.
Hyperinflation	A situation where the general price level is rising very rapidly.

In the red	Being in debt as a result of expenditure exceeding income.
Income	A flow of money that rewards factors of production for their services.
Income elasticity of demand	Measures of the response in demand to changes in income.
Incomes policy	A government policy designed to control factor incomes, most commonly wages.
Indirect tax	Taxes levied on goods and services which households only pay if they buy those goods and services.
Inelastic	Not responsive.
Inferior goods	Goods for which the demand tends to fall as peoples' incomes rise.
Inflation	A sustained increase in the price level.
Inflationary noise	The distortion of price signals caused by inflation.
Injections	Additions to the circular flow of income.
Interventionist approach	The process by which governments and other external agencies may intervene into the free working of markets, to promote efficiency.
Investment	Spending on capital goods.
Kyoto Agreement	International agreement to limit the emissions of greenhouse gases (not accepted by the USA).
Labour Force Survey	A household survey that collects a range of information on the labour force. In deciding who is unemployed from the responses given, this measure uses the ILO definition.
Leakages	Withdrawals from the circular flow in income.
Long-run aggregate supply	Total supply that can be produced with the full employment of resources.
Luxury goods	Goods that have a positive income elasticity greater than one.

Macroeconomic disequilibrium	A situation where aggregate demand and aggregate supply are not equal.
Macroeconomic equilibrium	A situation where aggregate demand equals aggregate supply.
Marginal tax rate	The proportion of extra income that is taken in tax.
Market clearing	The price necessary for all stocks of goods to be sold and all consumers satisfied.
Menu costs	Costs involved in changing prices in say, catalogues, due to inflation.
Merit good	Good which if left to market forces would be under-consumed and which has positive externalities.
Mixed economies	Economies involving a mix of private and public provision of goods and services.
Monetary policy	Government changes in the money supply, the rate of interest and the exchange rate.
Monopoly	In theory, this is when one firm produces the entire output of an industry. In UK law, this is when one firm produces more than 25 per cent of the total output of an industry.
Mortgages	Long-term borrowing, used to purchase property.
Multiplier (effect)	The process by which any change in a component of aggregate demand results in a greater final change in real GDP.
Natural conditions	Differing conditions of certain countries such as weather and landscape, which result in commodities that can be traded in areas not able to produce such things.
Negative equity	A situation in which property is worth less than any outstanding debts acquired through borrowing for its purchase.
Negative externality	Additional costs faced by a third party caused by the production of a particular good or service.

Net exports	The balance arrived at by deducting the value of imports from that of exports. This can be a positive or negative amount.
Non-renewable resources	Natural resources when used up cannot be replaced.
Opportunity cost	The best possible alternative that has to be given up as the result of a particular choice.
Output gap	The gap between potential and actual output.
Positive externality	Additional benefits enjoyed by a third party, caused by the production of a particular good or service.
Price controls	The imposition, usually by governments, of maximum or minimum price levels for particular goods or services.
Price discrimination	Charging different prices to different customers for the same product.
Price elasticity of demand (PED)	$\dfrac{\% \text{ change in quantity demanded}}{\% \text{ change in price}}$
Price elasticity of supply	$\dfrac{\% \text{ change in quantity suggested}}{\% \text{ change in price}}$
Price indexes	Measures of changes in the price level.
Price makers	Firms which have sufficient monopoly power to set prices.
Price mechanism	A means by which resources can be allocated between different and competing uses.
Private costs	Costs faced by the organisation responsible for producing a good or service.
Privatisation	Transfer of ownership from the public to the private sector.
Production possibility frontiers (PPF)	Different combinations of two goods or services which can be produced at a given time in a given economy.

Productive capacity	The maximum possible output that can be produced with existing resources and technology.
Productive efficiency	Producing goods and services at the lowest possible average cost.
Productivity	Output per worker/hour.
Public goods	Goods for which the principles of non-exclusivity and non-rivalry apply.
Quota	A limit on imports.
Recession	A fall in real GDP that lasts for at least six months.
Renewable resources	Natural resources which, when used, can be replaced.
RPI (Retail Price Index)	A weighted price index calculated by first finding out what people spend their money on. This is done by carrying out a Family Expenditure Survey. Price changes are checked throughout the country. The final stage is to multiply the price changes by the weights.
Short run aggregate supply	Total supply over the time period when factor prices are unchanged.
Shoe leather costs	Costs involved in moving money around in order to offset the effect of inflation.
Social benefits	Private benefits plus external benefits.
Social costs	Private costs plus external costs.
Social housing	Housing provided by the state or other agency as a merit good.
Specialisation	Concentrating on the production of a particular good or service, or on a particular stage of the productive process.
Substitutes	Goods which are similar. One good which can be consumed instead of another.
Supply curve	Shows the likely relationship between the price of a good or service and the quantity supplied. These curves usually slope upwards from left to right showing that as price rises, supply is also likely to rise, whereas if price falls supply is likely to fall.

Supply-side policies	Policies designed to increase aggregate supply by raising the efficiency of markets.
Surpluses	When more is produced at a given price level than will be consumed.
Sustainable economic growth	Economic growth which does not lead to the depletion of non-renewable resources.
Tariff	A tax on imports.
Tax relief	Allowances which can be given to firms and individuals which reduce the amount of direct taxes which have to be paid.
The Bank of England	The UK's central bank. Founded in 1694, it issues notes and coins and implements the government's monetary policy, including changing interest rates when it is thought appropriate.
The invisible hand	Adam Smith's notion that markets will automatically ensure an optimum distribution of resources.
Trade unions	Organisations of workers designed to protect pay and conditions of employment.
Trend growth	Expected increase in productive capacity over time.
Wealth	A stock of assets that have a financial value.
Weighted consumer price index	Changes in the prices of goods and services that people spend more on are given more importance than those on which they only spend a small amount.
World Trade Organisation (WTO)	An international organisation that promotes free international trade and rules on international trade disputes.